SOCCER UK
The Winning Team

Soccer Coaching
For
5 - 8 Year Old's

Published by
WORLD CLASS COACHING

First published July, 2002 by
WORLD CLASS COACHING 9205 W. 131 Terr, Overland Park, KS 66213 (913) 402-0030

ISBN 0-9718218-5-2

Edited by Mike Saif

WORLD CLASS COACHING would like to thank
worldofsoccer.com for the use of the graphics

WORLD CLASS COACHING

Published by
WORLD CLASS COACHING

Contents

UNIT ONE

The Coaching Process

A1 Attacking Player	Path of Player		Path of Dribble
D1 Defending Player	Path of Ball		Target Area

COACHING PROCESS

At the level that this book is based, success of the training session is not dependent upon your experience or knowledge of soccer, but how well you follow the principles of the Coaching Process.

Many beginner coaches in whatever the sport, make the fatal mistake of thinking that because they have played the game, coaching is therefore easy. Wrong! The most important aspect of putting on an effective coaching session is being able to organize the children, equipment and area effectively to ensure that the maximum use of the time is made.

Understanding and knowing the game is important and the higher the ability level you work with the higher level of knowledge and understanding is required. To be able to effectively coach you need to be organized, and this comes through good planning and evaluation. Time spent planning and structuring a session will have a great deal more impact on children than the coach who thinks he can turn up and produce a session off the top of his or her head.

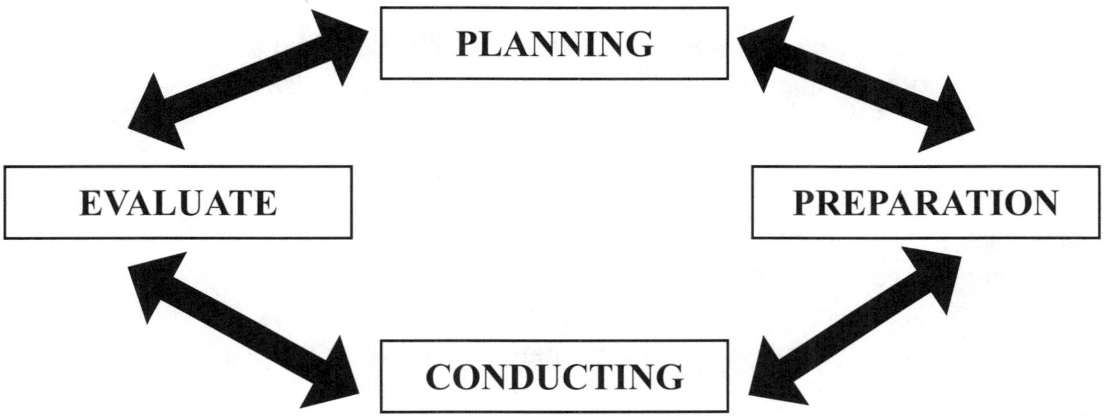

As you can see from the diagram above, the cycle is a two way model. Yes it is important to carefully plan the session so that it can be conducted effectively, but as you conduct the session you need to be flexible in your approach as you need to be constantly evaluating the session. As the session is taking place, you may need to re-plan in your head and make slight alterations to ensure it is successful. Remember not all children or groups are the same. What may work for one may not work for another.

Planning and Preparation

- To have an effective practical session you first must have SMELT it (see page 9)
- "Today's preparation determines tomorrows achievements". Arrigo Sacchi : Italian National Team Manager 1996
- "Funny, the more and more we prepare - the luckier we become!" Lou Holtz, Notre Dame University - Football Coach.

Check facilities and equipment

Conducting The Session

With the most difficult part out of the way, now it is time for the enjoyable part, delivering the sessions. Here are 4 simple steps to follow:

Step 1

- Ensure there is a purpose - it forms part of a long term strategy
- Long term strategy will provide short term objectives
- Identify what you want the players to learn in a logical sequence in relation to priority

Step 2

Consider

- Age and ability of the players
- Number of participants (do you need to split the group to ensure more players are involved more of the time) (16 = two groups of eight)
- Venue (can you use existing pitch markings)
- Equipment (more balls more touches)
- Appropriateness of activities (are they specific to game situations and the age they are for?)
- Progress from simple to complex (don't be afraid to take a step back).

Step 3

Consider when organizing players for practice:

- Number of players - ensure players are always active/receive adequate rest.
- Size and safety of area
- Equipment available (make use of the equipment where ever possible)
- When to progress activities (players may need more or less time than planned for)

Step 4

Provide explanations and/feedback. Adopt the "KISS" approach - Keep It Short and Simple.

- Use demonstrations as a visual tool for understanding.
- Ensure feedback is positive.
- Give clear and understandable information.
- Adjust information to suit the performer.

COACHING PRINCIPLES

The philosophy of this book isn't about coaching, rather structuring the sessions so that the children can educate themselves. However, it is important that the principles of coaching are followed:

Environment

It is essential that the area that you are working is constantly monitored and evaluated:

Is it safe?

Refer to the "SMELT" approach

Is it the correct size for the activity you are doing?

Does it allow the players to experience success, is it too small or too big?

Targets/Goals

To ensure that the players are motivated (SMELT approach) coaches should try to make the goals **SMARTER**.

Specific to the performance (e.g. how many crosses can you get in, in a game).
Measurable - how many crosses did you actually get in
Acceptable to the player - agreed by the coach and player
Realistic but challenging - the player must feel it is within their capabilities
Time - phased - e.g. during each half
Exciting so that the player feels a sense of achievement.
Recorded to enable players and coaches to monitor progress.

Role of the Coach

Coaching isn't about commentating and telling players what to do - It's about observing, allowing players to learn for themselves by putting them in an environment which allows them to learn.

By stepping back to observe the session without verbally or physically being involved in it will allow you to access the degree to which your session or players have met their aims and objectives. You should be on the outside looking in not the inside looking out. It is therefore essential that you position yourself to allow you to see all the areas and players.

EVALUATION

To ensure the success of a session you should continually be looking at ways in which it can be improved. Alternatively if something is successful it should be used again. Long term, this will allow you to assess the capabilities of the group or age of players that you are working with. Remember nobody can produce the perfect session, there are always ways it can be improved to allow it to work more effectively. Evaluating should be continuous throughout the session and not just at the end.

UNIT TWO

Planning and Organization

Planning The Session

Whether you are planning for a session, or longer term for a season, there are a number of principles, which can ensure safe, effective and enjoyable football. To help you remember the process, if you have planned correctly, you will have S.M.E.L.T. it first.

Safety

A Planning priority when working with young players is to ensure that they are working within a safe environment. The facilities that you use may not look dangerous, but it is vital that we recognize any potential dangers to ensure that accidents and injuries are reduced. As the Leader of activities you have a responsibility to ensure that players are safe and free of risk and harm.

Safety Guidelines to follow

- Check that the facility being used is appropriate for the activity and practices. Ensure that you are aware of the health and safety procedures for the facility.
- Check the area for dangerous objects (i.e., Cans, Glass and holes). Organize the area/pitch allowing for posts and roadways.
- Have a storage area or coned area for spare equipment, first aid kit, bibs, cones and drinks.
- Check all equipment before use ensuring that;

It is of the required standard and there are no damaged or broken items.

Specific guidelines of the manufacturer are followed when assembling equipment such as goals.

All equipment should be stored in a suitable place to ensure that any damage is limited. You should keep a record of all equipment. It is vital that all equipment is checked out and in following activities.

- Ensure access to drinks for fluid replacement is available.
- Ensure easy access to a Telephone.
- Ensure awareness of location
- Check participants equipment (Jewelry, Dress, footwear, shinguards etc)
- Maintain a register of participants, including contact addresses and telephone numbers.
- Knowledge of a participant's previous experience, and Medical conditions.

It is also vital that any activity is preceded by a structured warm up and finished with a cool down. Particular attention should be paid to those muscle groups to be used within the session.

Ensure activities and drills are within the physical capabilities of the group and try to avoid long periods of inactivity.

Motivation

1. Maintain interest through variety : utilize skill drills, practices and conditioned game situations.
2. Give plenty of positive feedback : ensure the children have a positive experience by using praise. Don't be slow in giving positive reinforcement when things go well.
3. Help players feel a sense of fulfilment : help them set short term and long term goals.
4. When working with children, keep the emphasis on enjoyment and skill development. Keep competition and winning in perspective.

Equipment

1. Have all equipment checked and ready - for example cones, balls, flags, etc.
2. Ideally the following should be available:

- An ample supply of balls. This is by far the most important item.
- One ball per player, or at worst one ball between two.
- Cones, witches hats, or event ice cream cartons, to mark out playing areas and goals
- Bibs, singlets or sashes, so that groups or teams can be identified by color.

Learning

1. REMEMBER an individual practice session should be part of a longer term plan.
2. Use mini game practices, which incorporate individual and team skills, as soon as possible.
3. Players learn through seeing, hearing and feeling - make sure you use all the senses.
4. Use conditioned games to ensure repetition and grooming of skills.

TIMING

1. Set a good example. Be there to start the session on time and make the first session fun so all the players want to be there and return.
2. Plan time allocations of various activities within the session to ensure the children's interest and attention is maintained. Ensure maximum participation; don't have children standing around for long periods of time.

Organizing a Session

When organizing a session the simplest approach to take is to think of a series of steps :

Step One
Identify what you want the players to learn. (Session topic)

Step Two
Select the skills, practices and modified games to be used. (The session plan)
Consider:

- Age
- Number of participants
- Venue
- Equipment
- Appropriateness of activities
- Progression from simple to complex

Step Three
Plan how to organize participants to practise the skill. (The progression)
Consider:

- Number of players
- Size and safety of area
- Equipment available
- Progression from one activity to another
- Enjoyment/fun of activities

Step Four - Planning
Plan the explanation and demonstration - "what to say and how to say it".

- Gain everyone's attention before starting
- Ensure that they can all see and hear you and that no one is behind you.
- Do not stop activity until you know what you are going to say
- Demonstrations are an effective way for focusing players' attention on what they have to do.
- You do not need to be able to play in order to demonstrate. The demonstration may be done in slow motion and in isolation. Alternatively, you can use one of the more competent players to show what you want practised:
- To introduce a technique, explain a particular point, or as motivation by highlighting a particular group working well.
- Instructions and explanations accompanying demonstrations should follow the KISS approach: "Keep It Short and Simple".
- Use a number of key words and phrases to highlight the main points and then allow for activity
- When demonstrating you may need repetition so that players understand what is required of them.

Step Five - Providing Feedback

- Feedback at this level should encourage and be non-technical
- Make sure feedback is positive
- Feedback should be clear and understandable. If appropriate, check that players understand what you are saying.
- Keep feedback as simple as possible with younger and less skilled performers.

Step Six - Evaluating the Session

- Evaluate every session before you plan the next one.
- Assess the players' development as well as your own effectiveness.
- Were the session goals achieved?
- Did the session run smoothly?
- Was interest maintained throughout?
- Did the session provide the players with an enjoyable learning experience?

UNIT THREE

Physical and Mental Development of 5 - 8 Year Olds

Physical Development

Young players cannot be treated as miniature adults. Many coaches believe they can run the same practices for young children as they would for adults. Some coaches even use the same drills they used when they were mature adults!

This is very dangerous as the young body has yet to develop fully.

As educators we must be acutely aware of what we can and cannot do with young children. First and foremost we must realize that the young skeletal system is very fragile. Any damage through direct contact (a kick) or through overstressing the bones (through high intensity practices) can result in problems throughout their lifetime. Any pain or discomfort within the skeleton should be taken very seriously. Discomfort is often felt in the legs, hips and around joints. If the player complains of discomfort ask them to sit out the practice and make sure their parents are aware of the problem. Suggest the child should see a specialist doctor if the condition is bad.

Spatial Awareness

How many times have you seen children play and you think how clumsy they are? The rate of bodily growth can affect the way in which a child moves as their body size is always changing. Spatial awareness, the body's ability to read external messages and move accordingly, develops slowly and the coach again requires patience.

When should I rest the children?

Take a break every fifteen minutes or so depending upon the temperature and intensity of your practice. The more intense or warm the environment, then the more often you should rest the players. Make sure that all of the players bring a water bottle to the practice.

Psychological stress

Always use positive feedback when making a point to the young players. Never make a child feel as if they have done something very wrong. Point out how they performed the skill and then suggest other ways of completing the task. Positive reinforcement will help the child and this can be displayed during practice and games by the coach and parents alike.

Children have a very short attention span, perhaps 4 -5 minutes at most or even less for some. Make the practice fun. Without fun the children will switch off and become disinterested in soccer.

Problem solving

Young children have yet to develop the mechanisms that allow them to solve complex problems. Soccer skills often require the transfer of brain messages to a number of bodily parts. Be patient, as the children will find it difficult at first to understand and complete a skill. Once the brain is 'in gear' with the body then the skill will be learned very quickly.

Mental Development

For effective coaching of children between the ages of 5 and 8 years of age it is essential to understand their level of understanding and thus where they may be in terms of mental development. Key considerations should be how mental process change during childhood, socially and in the process of decision making.

Coaches often assume that soccer encourages numerous aspects such as an aid to learning, development of teamwork, positive attitudes and fair play.

However, children may not necessarily perceive things in the same light, some may wish to participate with friends, some may use soccer as a form of competition, some may not be interested in any element, all dependent upon their level of mental development.

Social - A Child's Mind 5 to 8 years

During this period children are generally egocentric (self centred) and their physical characteristics will dictate how they feel about themselves. Individual skills and achievements of such to these children is seen as evidence of competence and very rarely will they compare their ability with other players.

During this period children will have a small circle of close friends but other children will become more significant in later years when they are able to compare their performances and analyze "who is best". Key influences at this age include role models, (generally soccer idols), older children and their peers.

Decision Making - A Child's Mind 5 to 8 years old

As children develop they become more apt at processing information they receive from a wide range of sources. Soccer being the nature of the game that it is, bombards its players with information from changing positions, calls from coaches, team mates and opponents, the playing surface and emotions that occur.

During this period children will have difficulty deciding which information to use and which is irrelevant. Children will be capable of responding to a small number of cues which is evident when they tend to follow the ball around the field and want to maintain possession without sharing it with team mates.

Coaching the Developing Child

Based on an understanding of the physical and mental processes of children between the ages of 5 and 8 years, the following guidelines should be followed:-

- Vary each coaching session
- Focus on the development of individual techniques
- Adapt the games to include small numbers (1 v 1, 2 v 2, 3 v 3) etc.
- Keep information short and simple (KISS)
- Limit information during match situations
- Demonstrate - A picture paints a thousand words
- Enhance decision making environment by increasing/decreasing number of players involved.
- Enhance decision making environment by increasing/decreasing size of the playing area
- Enhance decision making environment by increasing/decreasing the nature of the game (e.g. restriction to three touches per player)
- Use smaller sized equipment (e.g. size 3 footballs)
- Introduce coaching points one at a time

UNIT FOUR

Practices and Training Sessions

DEVELOPING CONTROL

Organization	Diagram	Coaching Points
Warm Up • In 2's players control & pass back to one another using different feet. • Every 5th pass player 1 passes beyond player 2 who turns & retrieves ball • Change roles & repeat	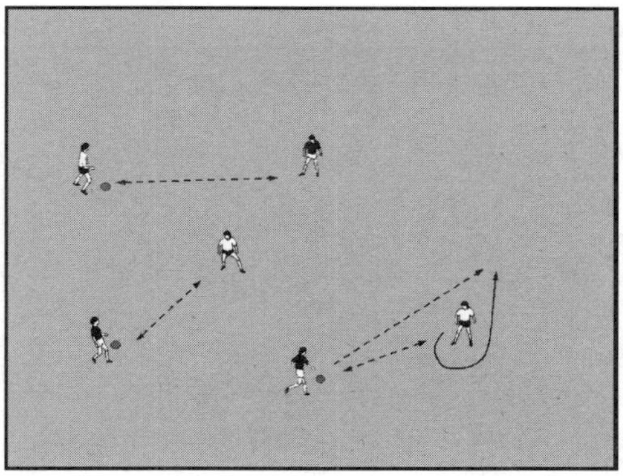	• Accuracy of control to prepare for pass • Identify surface for control early. • Use different surfaces to enhance "comfort" of control.
Technical • In 4's organize group into 1 receiver & 3 servers. Reduce number of balls to 2 per group • Receiver must control to allow pass to free server • Servers vary service (e.g. bouncing) to "challenge" receiver	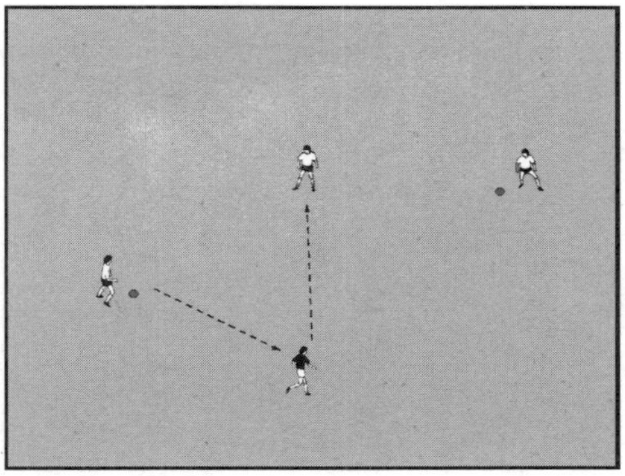	• Position body to increase options of control • Control in direction of next pass • Remain light on toes to allow quick movement.
Progression • In groups of 8, organize players into 2 middle/ 2 outside. • Dark's must keep possession by passing to any outside player • To score, players in middle pass to own 'outside' players		• Control ball away from opposition • Relax surface area on impact • Attempt ½ turn position throughout
Game Related Activity • Using 16 players play 4 v 4 with outside players as extras • Condition game to restrict middle players to control & pass to own outside players.	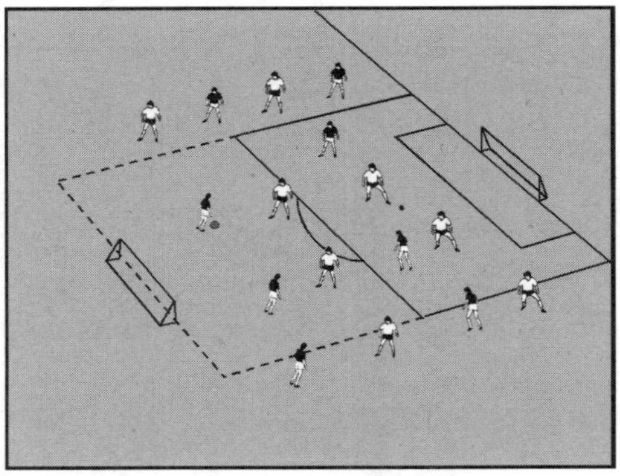	• Control ball away from opposition • Relax surface area on impact • Attempt ½ turn position throughout

<table>
<tr><th>Organization</th><th>Diagram</th><th>Coaching Points</th></tr>
<tr><td>Warm Up
Dark's and white's move around area passing to each other (must control before they pass). Introduce a competition to see how many passes and controls they can do in a set time period</td><td>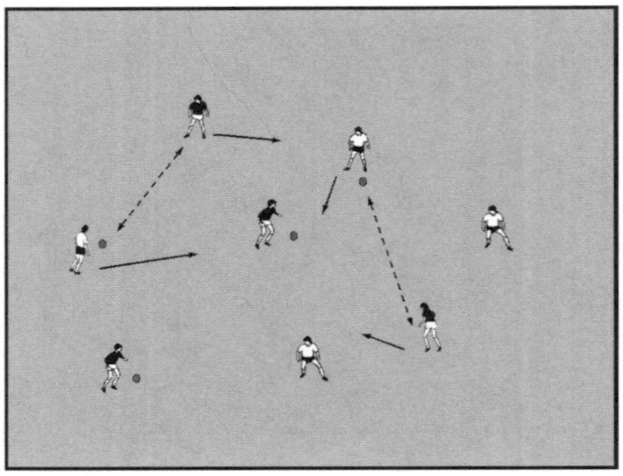</td><td>• Get in line with ball
• Use inside of foot
• Relax on contact</td></tr>
<tr><td>Technical
2 balls between 4. X1 & X2 with balls. X1 passes the ball to O. O has to control and pass back to X without ball (X3)
Variations of service
1) ball rolled
2) ball passed
3) ball thrown under arm</td><td>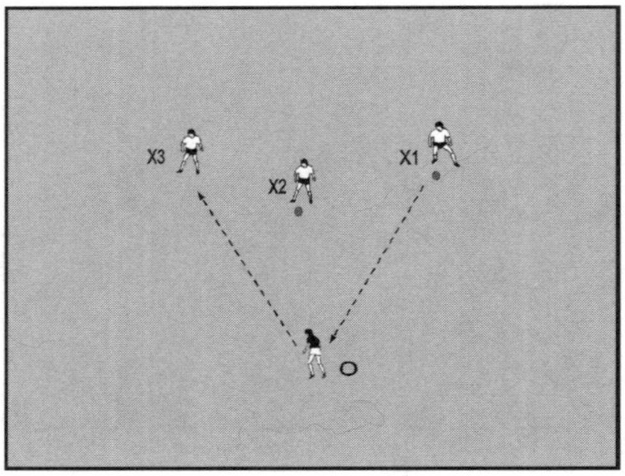
</td><td>• ready to receive ball
• receive and pass in 1 movement
• 2 seconds to receive and pass</td></tr>
<tr><td>Progression
As above but X's move around area to increase the learning environ-ment.</td><td>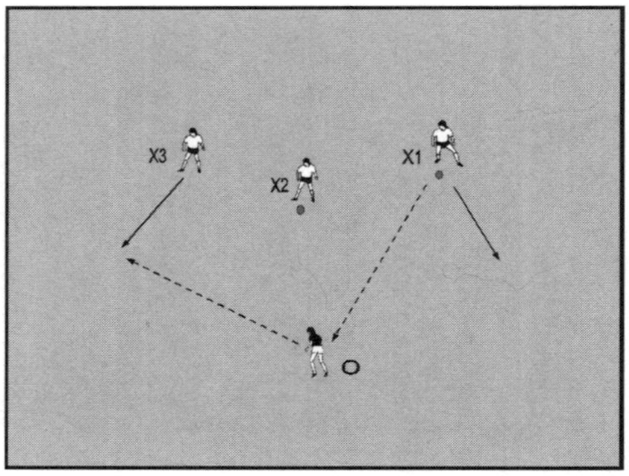
</td><td>• Keep head up, be aware of surroundings
• Control ball in direction of next pass
• Use both feet</td></tr>
<tr><td>Game Related Activity
Dark's v White's, 4 goals –
• To score players must pass between goal for outside player to control.
• Players then swap.
• Players must control ball and take it to side of the goal

As above and bring ball back into play in 1 movement</td><td>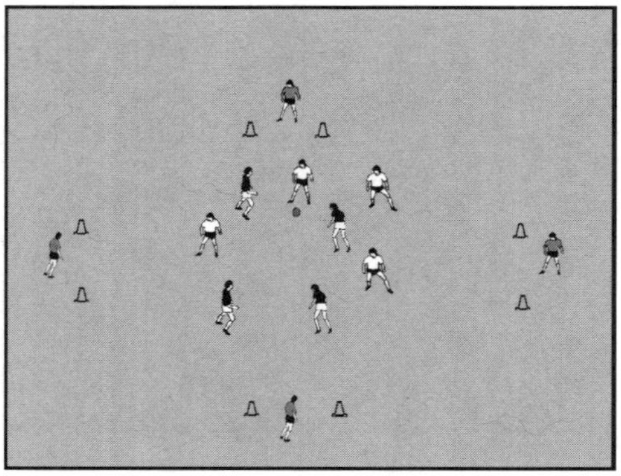</td><td>• Move in line with ball to receive
• Keep ball close to feet
• Use both feet</td></tr>
</table>

Organization	Diagram	Coaching Points
Warm Up • All players inside a square in pairs • Pass the ball between coned gates to each other (same gate to start) • Movement - How many passes can they do through all of the gates • How many passes within one minute • Can they beat their last score • Use both the left and right foot to pass & control	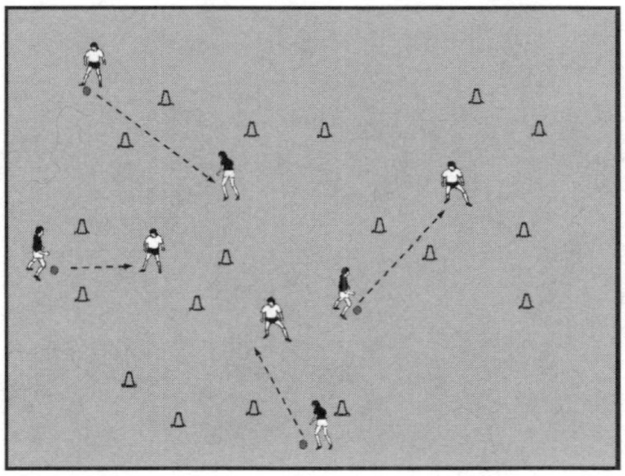	• Use the inside of the foot to pass • Move in line with the ball &Cushion the ball with the instep • Make the square & 'gates' bigger or smaller to help beginners and advanced players
Technical • Working in pairs • Side foot to partner standing opposite • Pass the ball to each other using the inside of the foot		• All points above • Do not let it hit the shin guards • Make the 'controlling' partner move from side to side • Go meet the ball (don't wait for it) • Arms out for balance & stay on toes for quick movement
Progression • Work in groups of four • 2 'controlling' players work side by side • Each controlling player faces their partner • Control the ball and pass back to their partner • Switch and face the opposite partner, receive and pass back • Switch and face original partner and continue		• All points listed above • As soon as they control and pass the ball, be aware and turn quickly to await the pass from their other partner • Remain on toes
Game Related Activity • Normal field size • No goalkeepers • 5 passes must be completed before the team can shoot • Extra points awarded if they pass into the corners of the goal marked out with cones		• All points listed above • Awareness that passing helps the team score goals • Pass into the net

Organization	Diagram	Coaching Points
Warm up Players are organized into pairs. One player stands still and acts as a server. Player two travels from server to server receiving passes	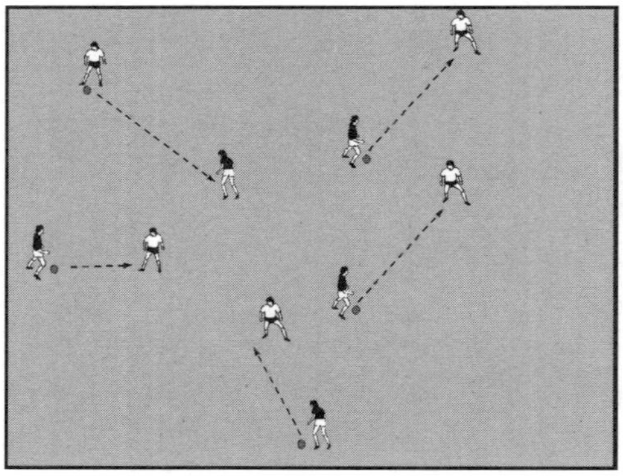	• Get in line with the ball • Offer the controlling surface • Cushion the ball by relaxing the foot.
Technical Give each player a number. Players pass the ball in sequence, i.e 1 to 8	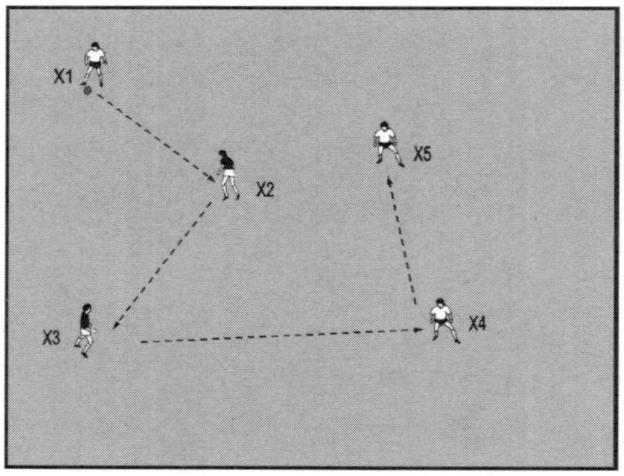	• Keep your head up • Control in the direction you wish to pass • Angle foot for direction
Progression Add an extra ball to the practice offering more testing environment.	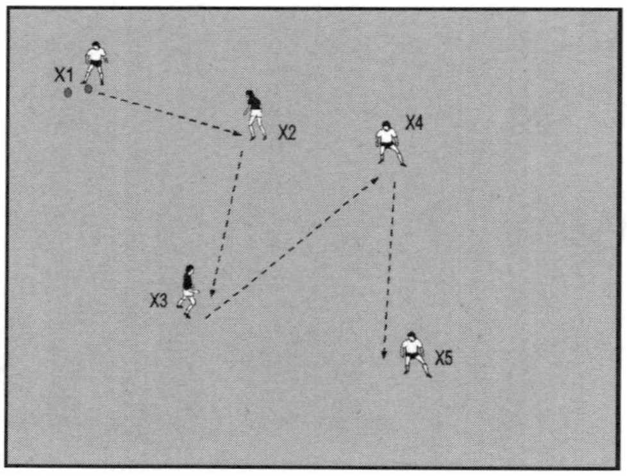	• Move towards the ball • Choose controlling surface early • Keep your eye on the ball
Game Related Activity Normal soccer rules apply. Each player must take two touches before passing.	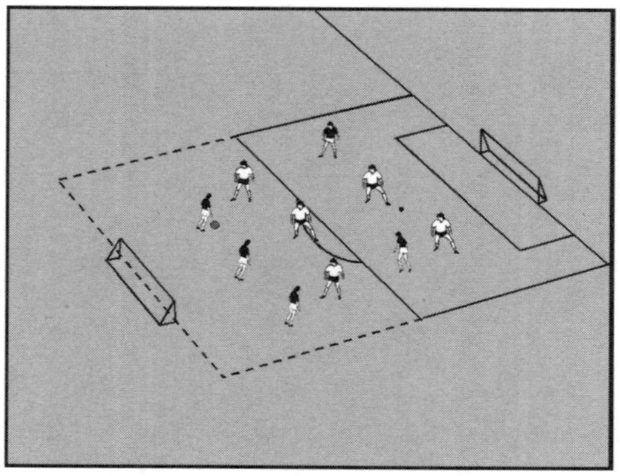	• Create space by moving wide • Use your body to shield the ball • Control the ball away from danger

DEVELOPING PASSING

Organization	Diagram	Coaching Points
Warm Up • 16 players move around area, 8 with balls passing receiving as they move • Players must take 1 touch then 2 then 3 & repeat each time they touch the ball	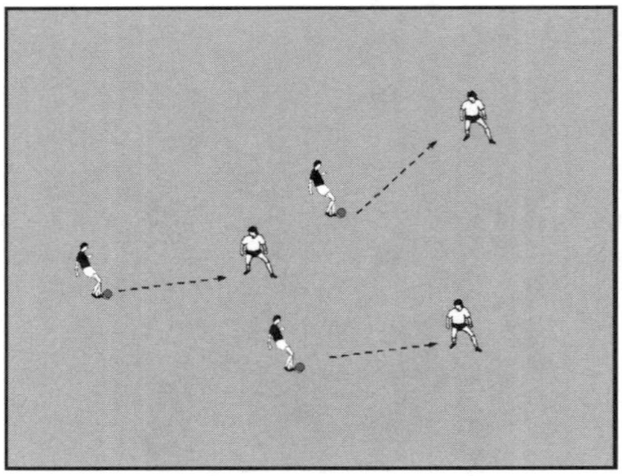	• Pass accurately • Use correct weight when passing first time • Use both feet
Technical In 2's in same area, players attempt to score goals by passing ball to hit other team's balls whilst keeping possession.	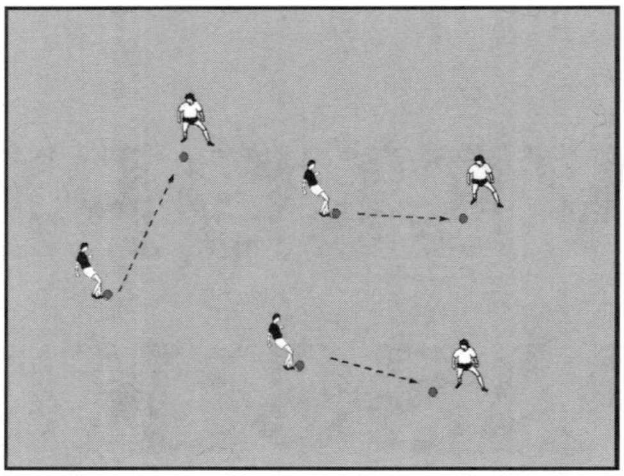	• Identify when to pass first time to partner to avoid ball being hit • Angled approach when preparing for strike • Use different surfaces where appropriate
Progression • In 4's in same area players attempt to knock balls off cones • 1 defender is placed in each zone to prevent goals being scored. • 6 passes also equals 1 goal	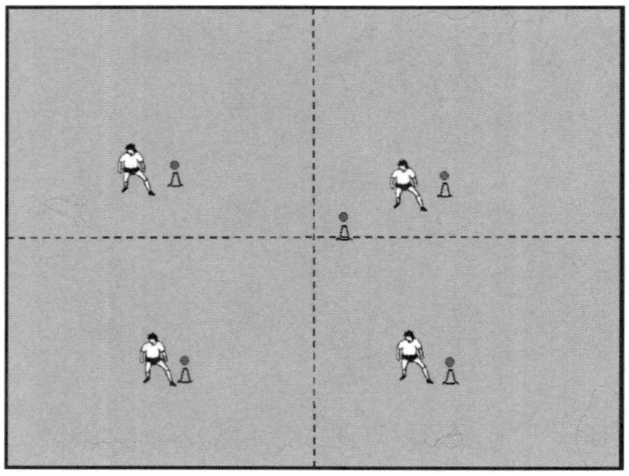	• Move ball quickly when goal is free • Remain composed when in possession
Game Related Activity • 6 players are organized into 2 dark's, 2 white's & 2 grey's • Players score in end goals and/or through 3 sets of cones randomly positioned. • grey's play for both teams	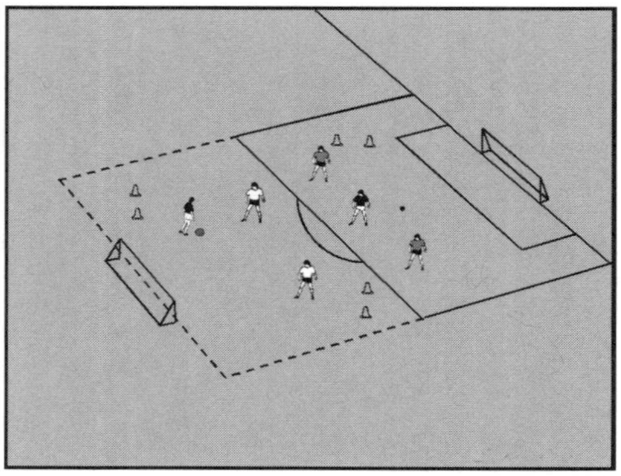	• Identify free players early • Vary passes depending on distance

Organization	Diagram	Coaching Points
Warm Up Players in pairs. Each pair makes a square with 4 cones, each cone a different color. Dark and white pass it back and forth. Upon command (color of cone). Players without ball must run around cone	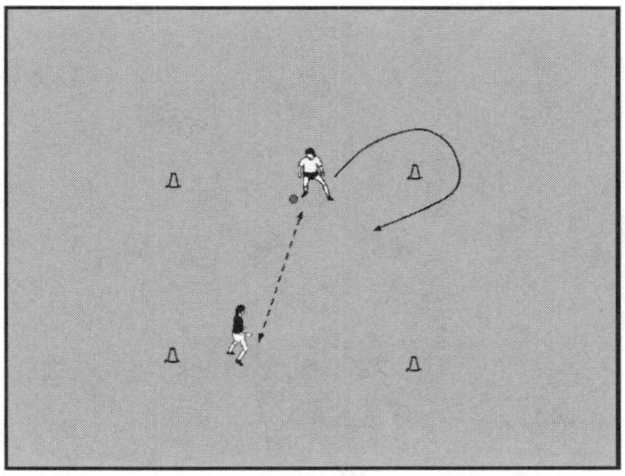	• Use inside of the foot • Non kicking foot to the side of the ball • Angled run up
Technical 1) White has to try and pass the ball to 1 of dark's cones and get it as close as they can without touching it. Closest wins. 2) White passes the ball to imaginary line between dark's cones and chases after it. The object is to catch the ball at the line without slowing down	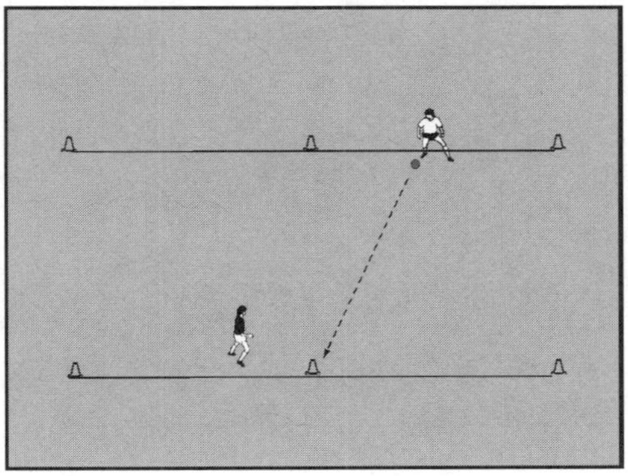	• Accuracy of pass • Pace of pass • Follow through
Progression Set up as above, players must pass from line and try and hit an opponents cone for a point. 1) Defender is static 2) Defender can move	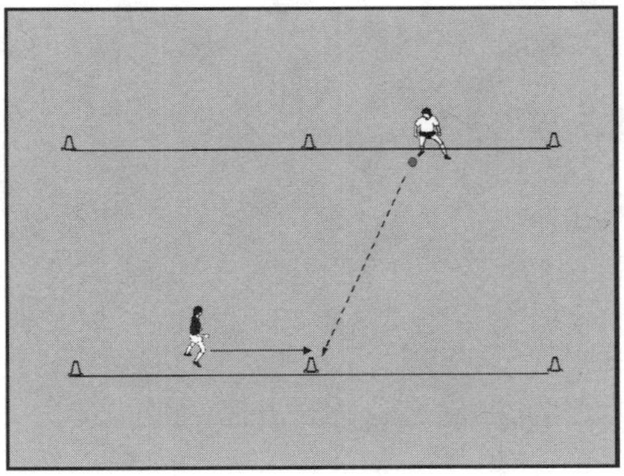	• Disguise pass • Pace / accuracy • Control and pass in one movement
Game Related Activity • Dark's v white's 3 passes = 2 goals • Goal = 1 goal	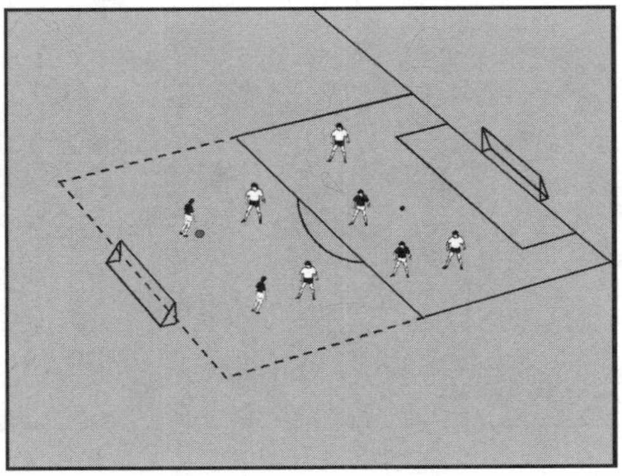	• Encourage players to pass • Pass / score

Organization	Diagram	Coaching Points
Warm Up • Group of 10 players divided into 4 pairs and two individuals. Players working in pairs must hold hands and not split apart at any time • The two individuals have a ball each and attempt to pass and hit the pairs (space invaders) below the knee • Players must remain within the square. If hit, the players step out of the area until the next game • Alternate pairs & individuals	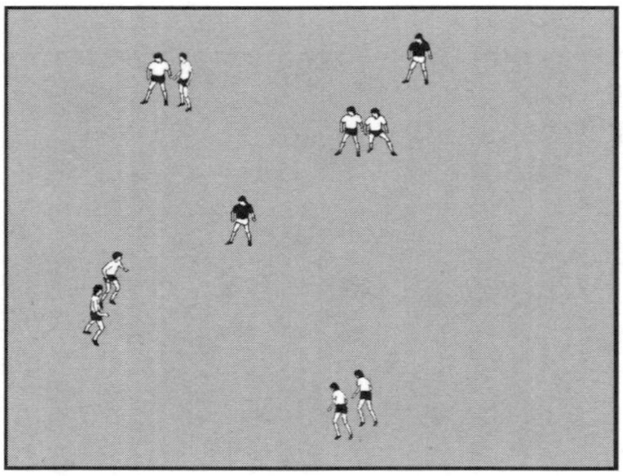	• Accurate instep passing • Point non-kicking foot towards target and next to the ball • Encourage passing into the line of the moving target • Head over the ball • Do not use toes
Technical • Players work within the same pairs as above • Stand opposite each other with one ball • Place 3 cones half way between the players • Players attempt to knock the cones over • 2 points scored for hitting the side cones and 5 points for hitting over the centre cone	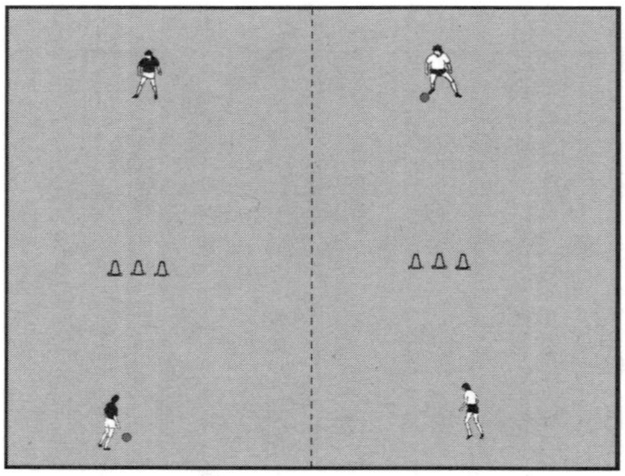	• All points above
Progression **'Where's Coach'** • Each player has a ball • Coach moves around the grid (with a separate helper if required) and opens their legs to form a tunnel • On seeing this players attempt to pass through the tunnel	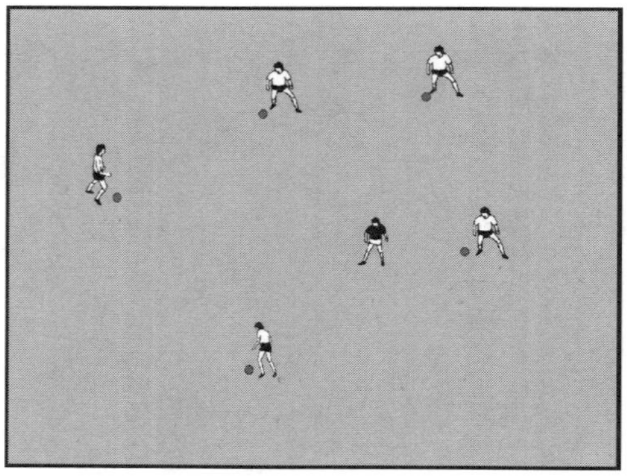	• All points above • Weight of pass is important as the ball needs to remain within the area • Head up to avoid collisions and watch coach • Movement - near to coach to make passing easier
Game Related Activity '5 goal game' • Equal teams • Players can score into any goal if they pass through the goal to a team mate • If the ball goes out of the area restart with a kick in (pass) • 2 points scored for passing through the corner goals and 1 point for passing through the centre goal	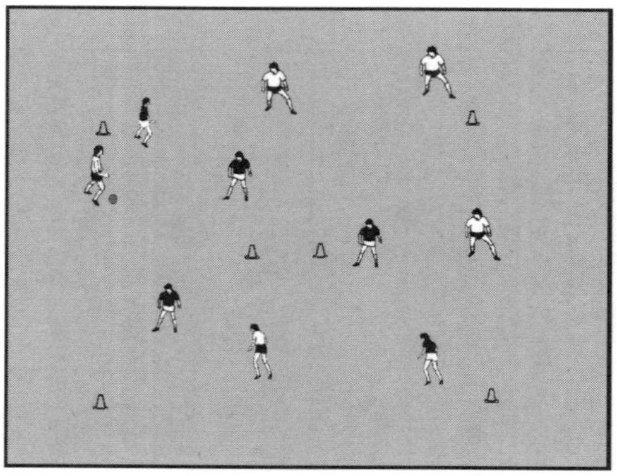	• All points above • Movement into space to receive a pass • Communication • Passing throughout the area • Good technique

Organization	Diagram	Coaching Points
Warm Up In pairs pass the ball through as many cones/goals as possible in two minutes.	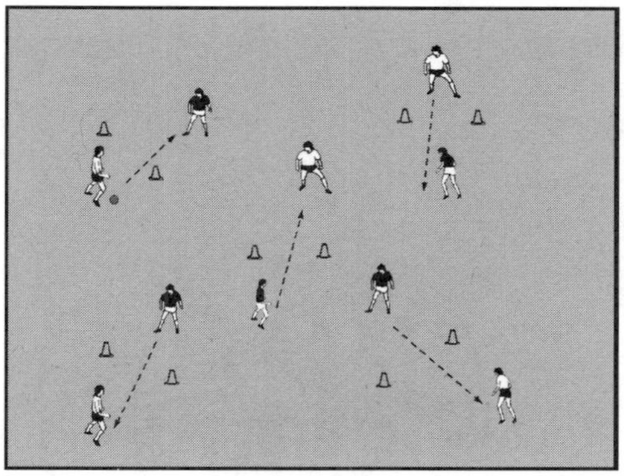	• Use the inside of the foot to pass. • Point your non-kicking foot at the target • Follow through to gain power
Technical Players are organized into groups of four. Players practice by passing the ball clockwise and alternatively anti-clockwise.	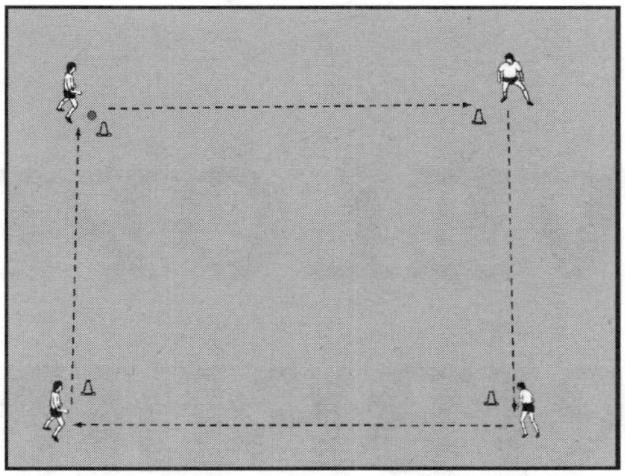	• Control the ball in the direction you want to pass • Keep your head up to see your target • Step through the ball to gain momentum
Progression Within the same organization players can: a. Pass in any direction b. The next most passes in two minutes wins.	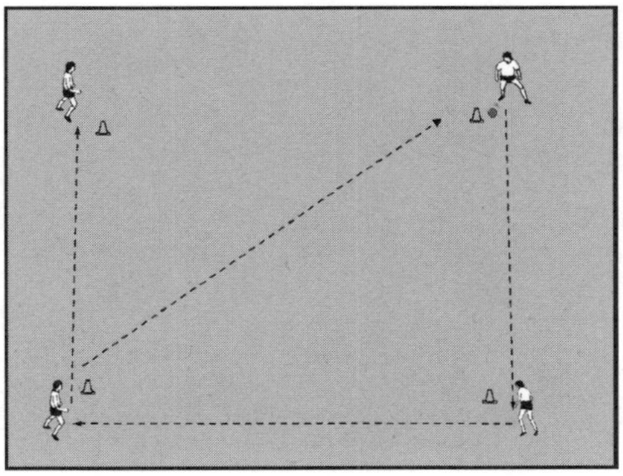	• Move towards the ball to gain control early. • Choose your target as the ball travels toward you • Keep your body over the ball to keep the ball on the floor
Game Related Activity Play a small sided game from 3 v 3 to 8 v 8. Score by passing through the small goal or by completing six passes without the other team touching the ball.	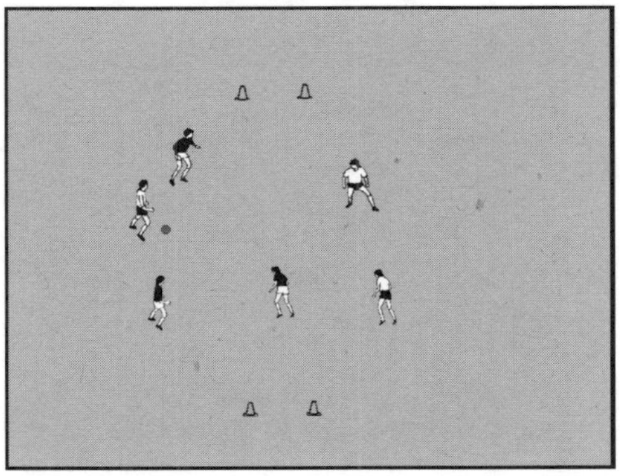	• Try to find space to receive a pass. • Pass to players in space. • Give a pass you would like to receive by monitoring the weight of the pass

DEVELOPING DRIBBLING

Organization	Diagram	Coaching Points
Warm Up • 16 players dribble around area with a ball • Upon command players - use right foot only - use left foot only - use inside of both feet - use outside of both feet - combine all of the above		• Keep head up • Maintain close control of ball
Technical • 16 players are organized into 4's positioned in corner boxes with 4 balls each. • Upon command 1 player from each team at a time must retrieve a ball from a different box until 1 team has 6 balls.	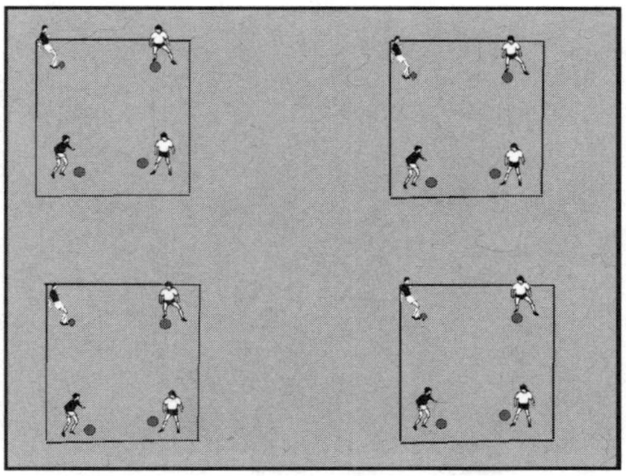	• Change direction & speed • Be aware of other players
Progression • Players repeat above game with 1 defender from each team in middle zone attempting to prevent access.	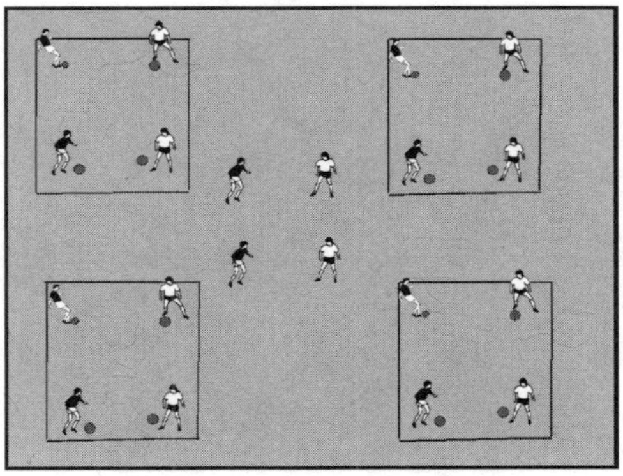	• Use different feet & surfaces to "pass" defenders • Change speed when beyond defenders
Game Related Activity • 8 players play 4 v 4 only • Player with the ball can enter side zones to dribble freely • Goals can be scored by dribbling through additional goals randomly placed.	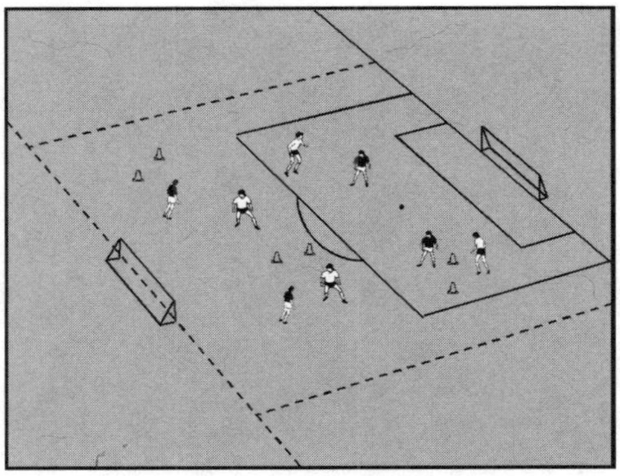	• Dribble on every 1 v 1 occasion • Keep head up to know when dribbling is appropriate

Organization	Diagram	Coaching Points
Warm Up • Dark's have ball • Dark's follows White's through the goals. • Upon command players swap roles.	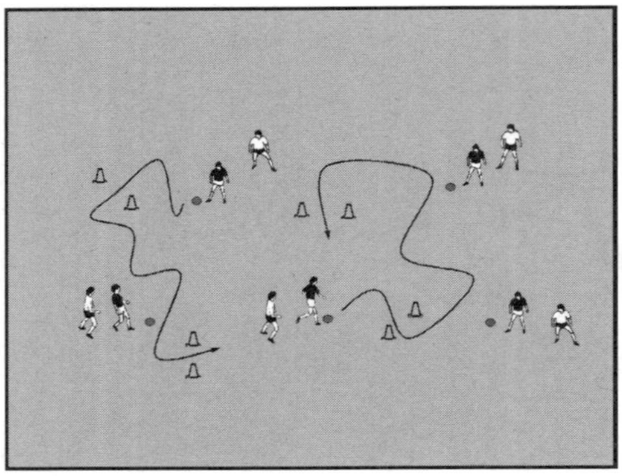	• Big toe little toe dribbling (inside and outside of foot) • Keep ball close • Head up
Technical • As above teacher holds up either a Red, yellow or Green cone • Red = stop • Yellow = different skill (coach chooses) • Green = Go	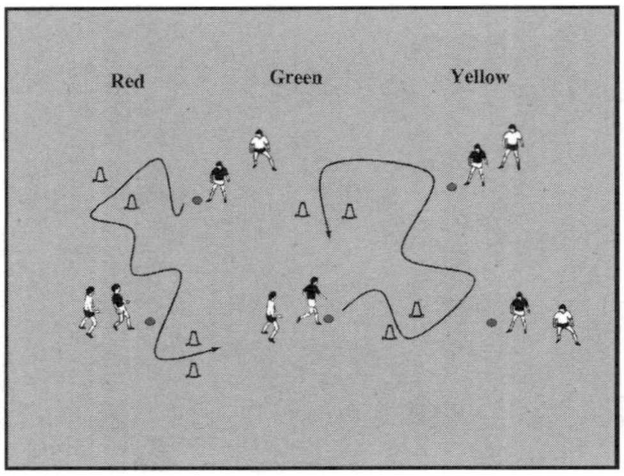	• Change direction • Use both feet • Awareness of space
Progression • Players work in pairs. White's (with ball) follow dark's. • When green cone is shown, dark's have to try and lose white's. • When the red cone is shown players have to stand still, dark's open their legs and white's have to try and pass the ball between them.	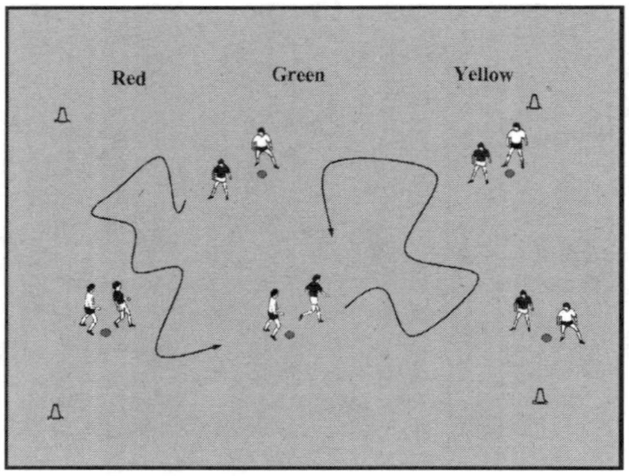	• Change pace • Ball under control • Avoid other players
Game Related Activity Dark's v white's • Players can either score in the goal for 1 point or dribble and stop the ball in the corner for 2 points	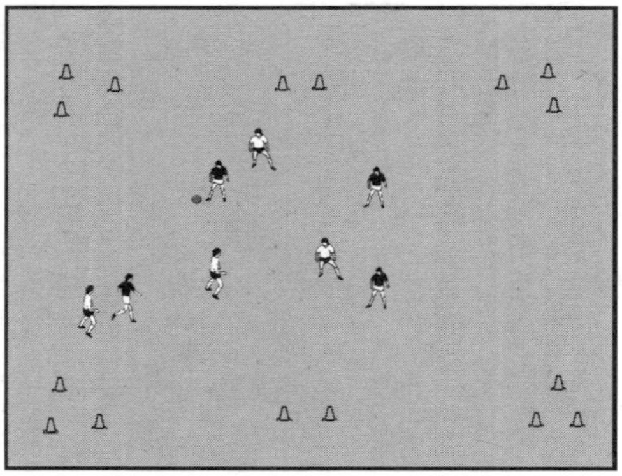	• When to dribble when to pass • Attack space • Change of pace

Organization	Diagram	Coaching Points
Warm Up • Group split into 2 teams • Players stand at each end line facing the opposite team • Place a ball behind each player on the line • On the command go the players run into their opponents half and dribble the ball back to their end line. • Continue until the coach says stop • The winning team has the most number of balls on their line • Don't count those in transit	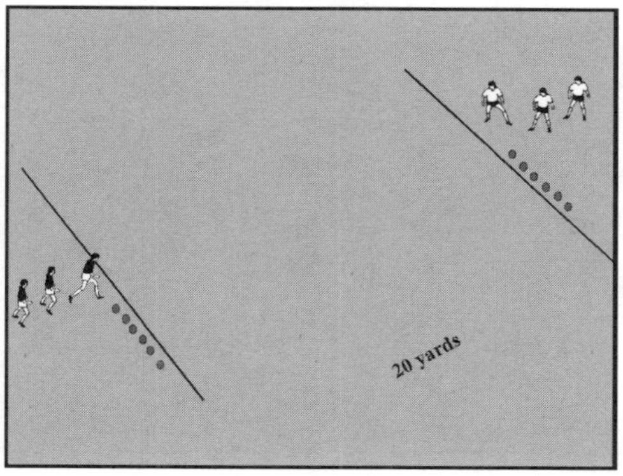	• Head up to avoid collisions • Keep the ball close by using the inside and outside of the foot to dribble • Remain on toes
Technical • Players work in pairs, one dribbling a ball and the other chasing • (Max of 3 pairs per area) • Dribblers start anywhere inside the square • Dribblers attempt to dribble around every cone before the chasers can tackle the ball from them • Chasers can only hop on one or two legs	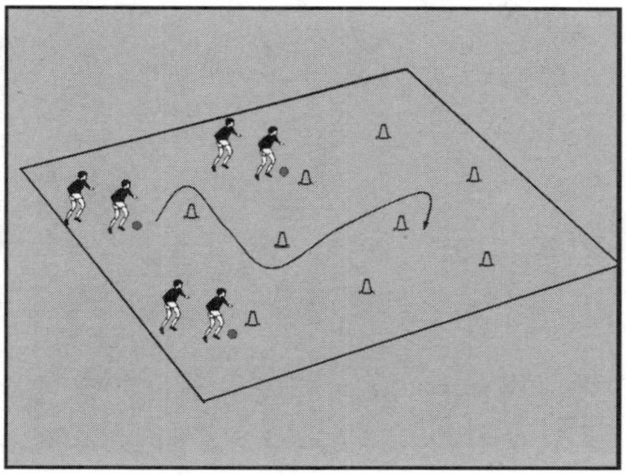	• All points above • Dribbler changes direction by using the inside and outside of the foot (big toe/little toe) • Bend legs to move from side to side quicker
Progression 'Gladiator Challenge' • Split the area into 3 areas • Place a defender in each area • Every player attempts to dribble through each area without being tackled • Defenders must hop		• As above • Concentrate on technique and not speed • Big toe/little toe to change direction
Game Related Activity • Split the group into 3 equal teams • No goals • Score by dribbling and stopping the ball on the opponents end line • Rotate teams	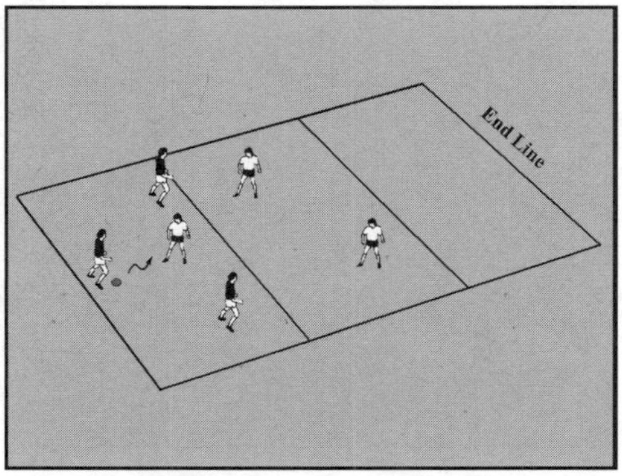	• As above • Concentrate on technique and not speed / numbers of goals scored

Organization	Diagram	Coaching Points
Warm Up All players dribble within a designated area. Players are instructed to avoid touching any of the cones set out.	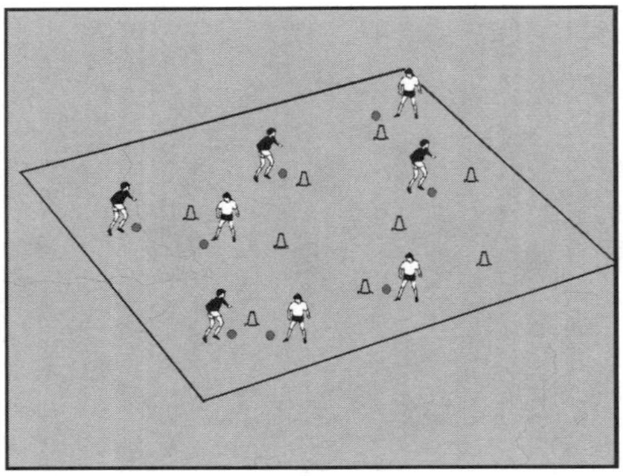	• Keep your head up • Keep the ball close to your feet • Take plenty of touches • Ask the players to perform a fake or move of their choice
Technical Players are organized with a ball each. Players are instructed to dribble within their designated area. On the coaches command players switch areas by travelling across the empty zones.	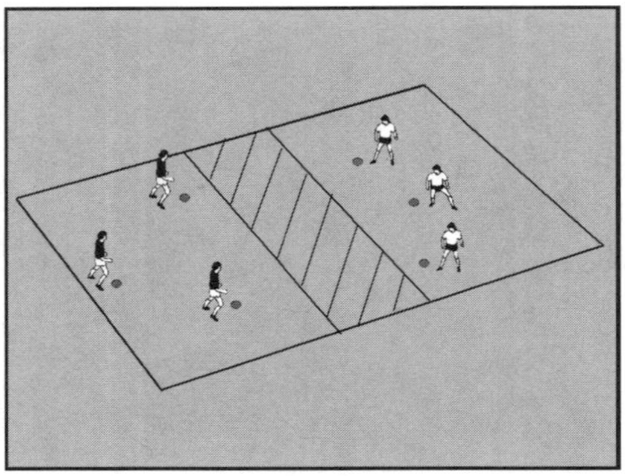	• Keep the ball moving • Keep your head up • Change zones by moving quick into space • Accelerate into space
Progression • Add a defender to 'empty zone'. All players have two minutes to cross the zones as many times as possible without losing possession. • Retrieve ball and continue if the defender kicks it away.	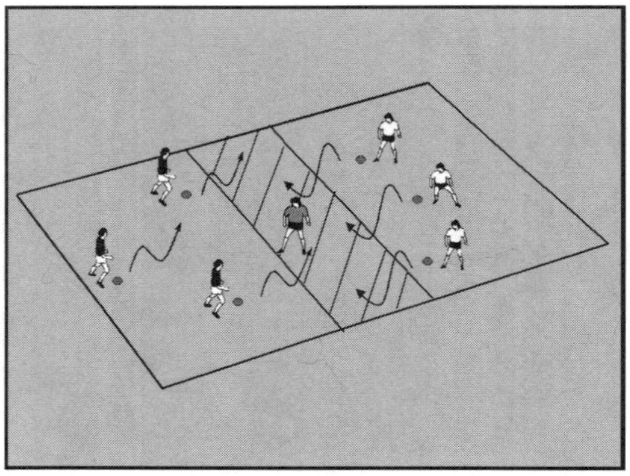	• Keep your head up • Speed up to attack free space • Bend your knees to change direction if required
Game Related Activity Players are separated into two teams. Score by dribbling through the goals.	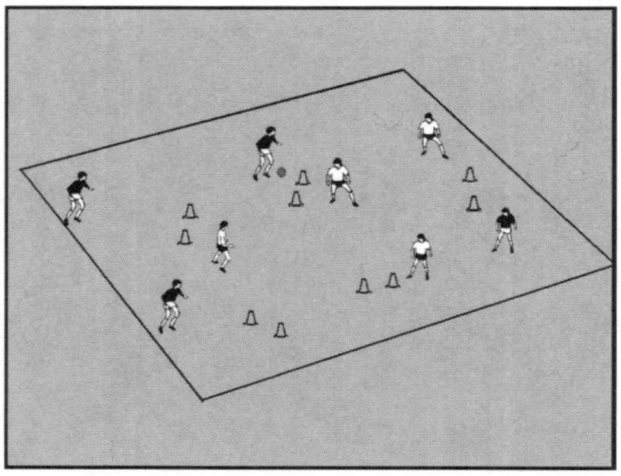	• Spread out to create space. • Speed up to attack space available. • Slow down when close to goal to ensure a 'score'

DEVELOPING RUNNING WITH THE BALL

Organization	Diagram	Coaching Points
Warm Up • 16 players with balls run with ball in counter-clockwise direction around circle • Upon command players - - change direction - use different feet - stop ball & continue • running with ball of player in front	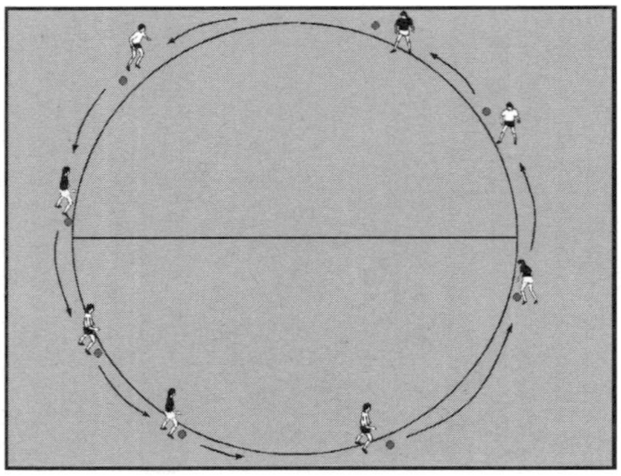	• Ball out of feet • Head up • Maintain control
Technical • In 4's players position themselves in groups around circle (clockface) • Each group pretend that they are positioned at 12 o clock. • Upon command players 1 at a time dribble to 10 o clock, 5 o clock etc.	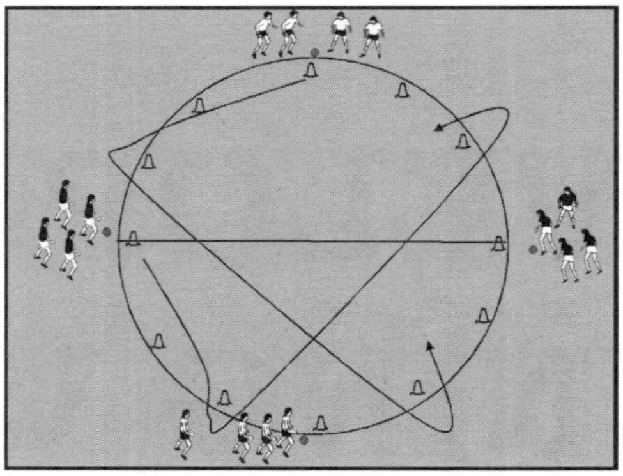	• First touch out of feet • Build up speed whilst maintaining control
Progression • Using same area 1 player from each team enters the circle to act as defenders • Repeat activities • Defenders begin by hopping	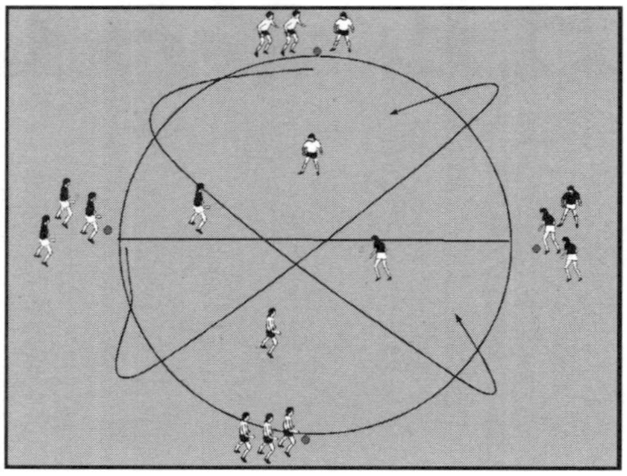	• Maintain close control until speed can be generated. • Change direction at speed.
Game Related Activity • 8 players are organized into 4 v 4 in zones • Players can enter other zones with ball only	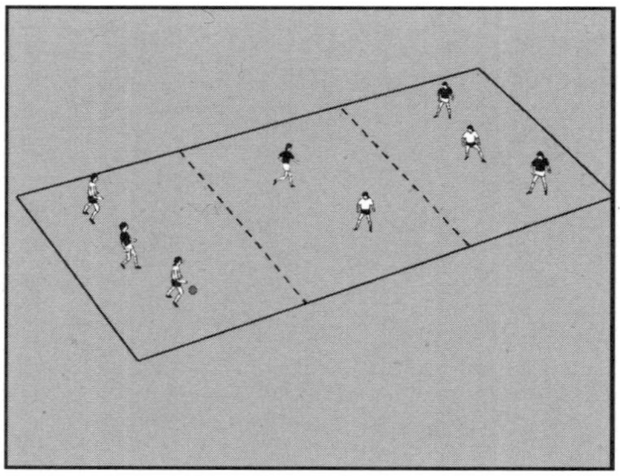	• All of above.

Organization	Diagram	Coaching Points
Warm Up • Players in a square. Half with the balls half without. • Players with the balls must run the ball to players without. • Players without the ball take the ball.		• Ball out of feet • Use laces • Less touches
Technical • In pairs dark's with balls white's with out. Dark's dribble the ball around. • On the command "change" dark's stop the ball leave it and carry on running around area white's find a ball and dribble. • When a coach calls out a number player with ball must take it to that side. Player without ball goes to opposite side.		• Head up • Avoid other players • Change of direction
Progression • As above but add skills (toe taps) that players have to perform. • On command, players without balls have to beat players with ball to the sideline.		• Move at speed • Ball under control • Head up
Game Related Activity Dark's v white's To score a goal ball must be run into end zone and stopped		• Attack space • Ball out of feet • Under control

Organization	Diagram	Coaching Points
Warm Up **'Fighter Planes'** • Each player has a ball and dribbles around the coned area • Dribble with arms out wide (wings) • Avoid contact with other fighter planes		• Use inside and outside of foot (shout big toe…little toe to help) • Keep the ball close & head up to avoid collisions • Change pace/direction
Technical • Players work at the same time as their partner - everyone with a ball • Player works towards their partner • Dribble to a centre cone, turn and repeat • Include extra cones for the players to dribble around before reaching the centre cone	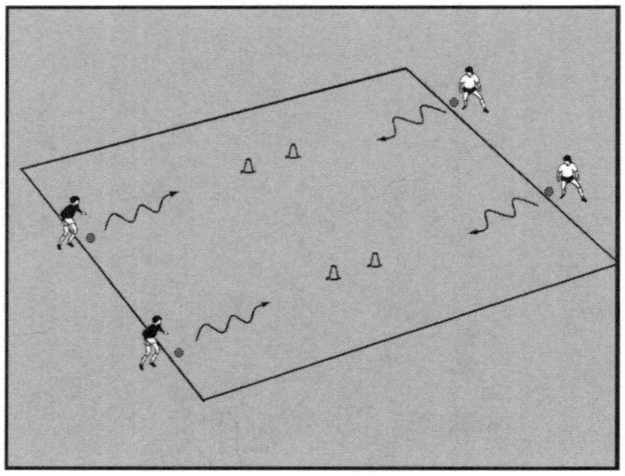	• All points listed above
Progression • Working in same pairs • Player starts with the ball on the end line • Player passes to partner (standing 5 yards away) who then turns and runs towards the opposite endline • After passing and the partner has turned, the player chases his partner but does not tackle • Dribbler moves forward cutting the ball from side to side & changing pace	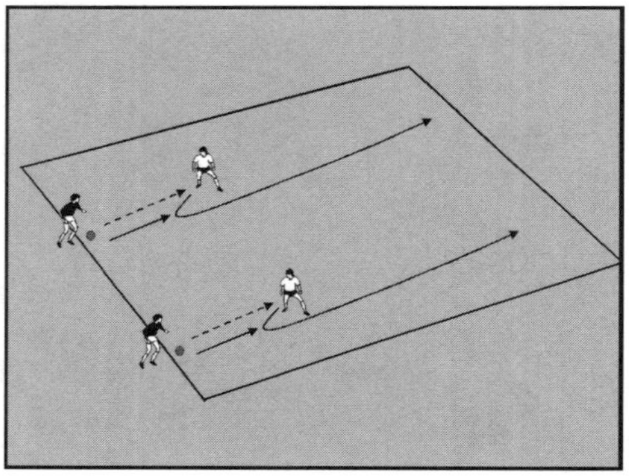	• Change of pace • Close control • Dribbler cuts from side to side
Game Related Activity • Teams split into 4 v 4 • No goalkeepers or 'goals' • Players attempt to dribble the ball over their opponents end line to score • **Encourage passing and dribbling**		• Dribble into space • Change direction when dribbling • Head up • Balance • Change pace when dribbling

Organization	Diagram	Coaching Points
Warm Up Set out four numbered areas with cones. Players have a ball each and dribble around a designated area. On the coaches command, players race towards and into a set area.	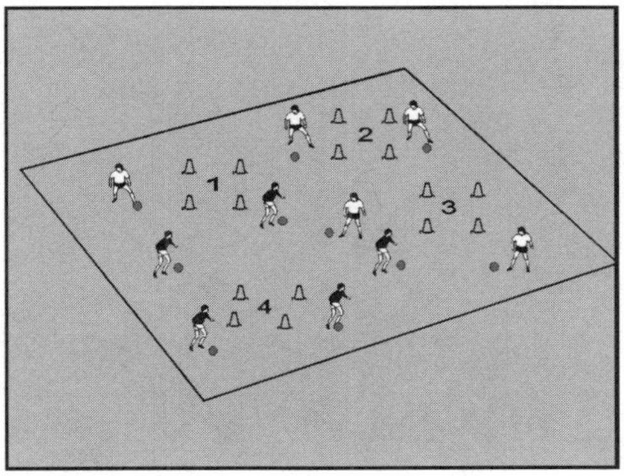	• Keep your head up • Move the ball out of your feet • Use you laces to move in a straight direction.
Technical Players are organized into small groups facing each other. Players take it in turns to run with the ball.		• Control the ball out of your feet • Arms out for balance • Look ahead at your target
Progression Players are organized into pairs facing a goal. On the coaches command the front player runs with the ball to score chased by a defender. Switch groups so everyone has a turn.	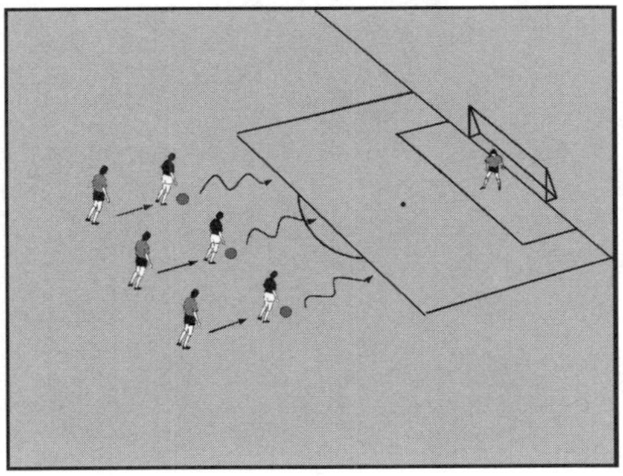	• Move the ball in the direction of the goal • Use your laces to move the ball • Move at speed to avoid being tackled
Game Related Activity Play a normal game but with side channels. If players move into a channel they can't be followed and can travel freely.	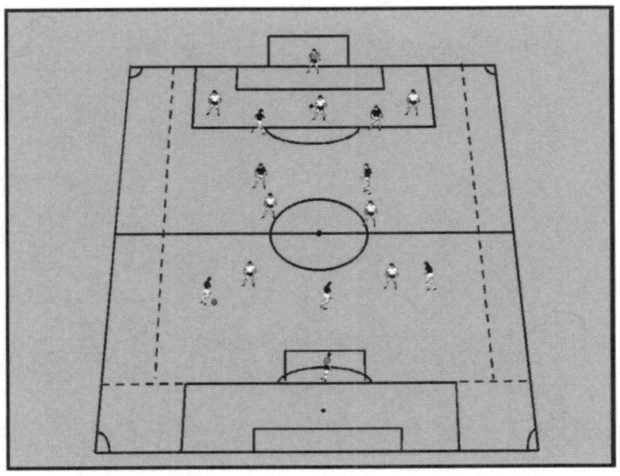	• Keeps your head up so you can attack space • Move quickly to take advantage of space • Only use the channel if there is no other opportunity to run with the ball.

DEVELOPING TURNING

Organization	Diagram	Coaching Points
Warm Up Players are given a ball each and instructed to dribble around an the area. When players approach a cone they perform a turn of their choice.		• Keep the ball close • Keep your head up • Control the ball using the inside/ outside of the foot
Technical Separate the players into four groups. Players are instructed to dribble towards a designated cone and perform a turn before returning to their group.	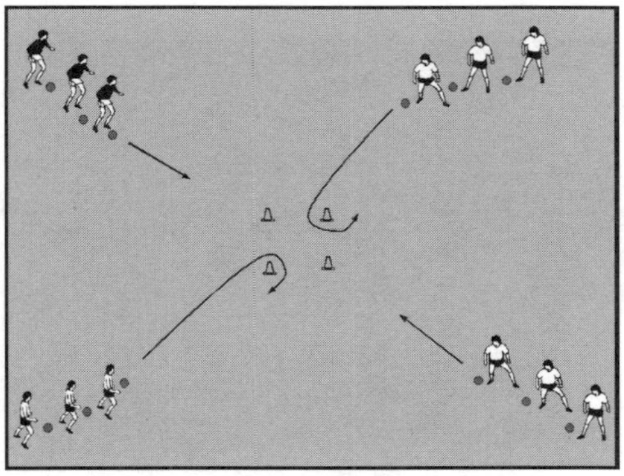	• Slow approach • Bend your knees on turning • Accelerate away • Turn in a small area
Progression Separate the group into pairs in a 10 x 10 yard area. Players have a ball each. Play a game of tag. A specified player aims to tag the others (or his partner) who attempt to avoid being tagged by using turns. Play for 60 seconds then switch roles.		• Keep the ball moving • Turn at a safe distance from an opponent • Get the ball out of feet to avoid escape • Dribble with head up to avoid collisions • Quick look behind before turning
Game Related Activity Organize the group into two teams. Normal game rules apply, Teams score extra goals by performing successful turns.	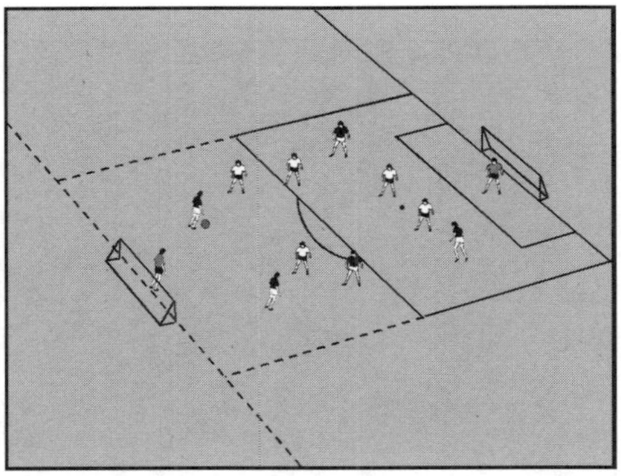	• Find space • Try to turn into space • Protect the ball from opponents by keeping your body in between the two

Organization	Diagram	Coaching Points
Warm Up • Dark's and white's move around area passing ball. • When they come to a cone they must turn and change direction	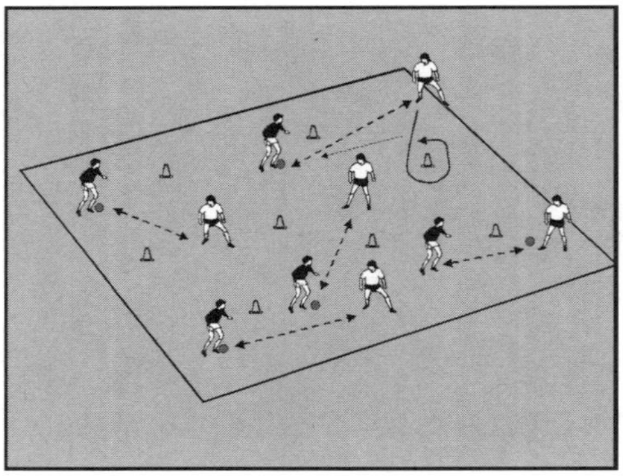	• Non kicking foot to side of ball • Turn and follow direction the ball is moving • Change speed
Technical • Dark's and white's pass ball between themselves (between cones). • White's move the ball a short distance and perform a turn and then pass back to dark. 1) Player performs turn and finds another partner 2) How many passes can each player make	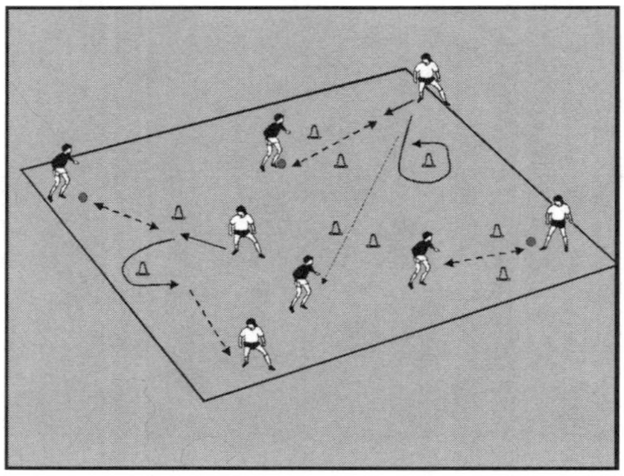	• Exaggerate fake movement • Ball remains under control • Change of speed
Progression As above. • Add 2 defenders whose job is to stand in between cones to stop pass (no tackling). • Players must turn and find another partner to make a pass with	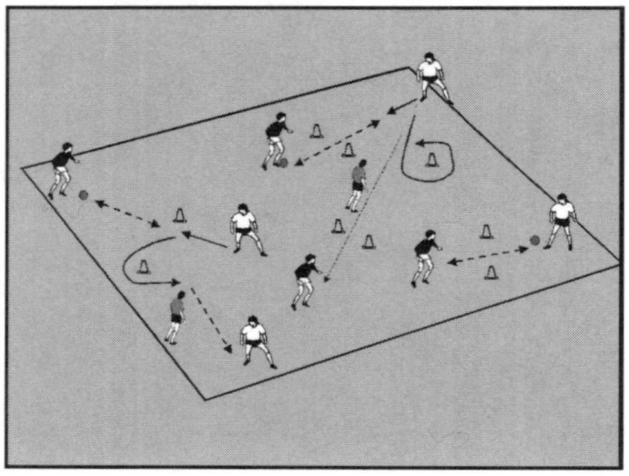	• Decision pass or turn • Turn into space • Change of speed
Game Related Activity • 4 areas in corner of pitch (player in each 2 dark's 2 white's). To score a goal players must pass ball to team mate in corner area. Players then swap over. • On receiving ball players must perform a turn • Players in area bring ball back into playing area on receiving and swap.		• Attack goal with least defenders • Keep head up • As above

Organization	Diagram	Coaching Points
Warm Up • All players within the coned area • Players run around the area awaiting the call 'turn' from coach • On the call of a number the players must complete that number of turns, stop their ball and then run to another ball and continue dribbling		• Players use the inside & outside of their foot to move the ball • Players must look over their shoulder before turning • Keep the ball close at all times • Awareness, look for the 'free' ball
Technical • Players work in pairs • Players alternate go's • Run to the first cone and complete a turn • Run back and stop the ball on the line for their partner to go • Pretend the cone they are running to is a defender and turn before the cone	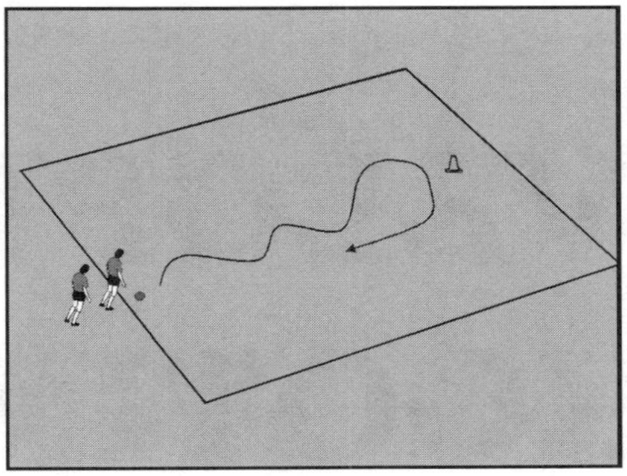	• All points listed above Use the following turns: • Stop • Drag back • Cruyff • Inside hook • Outside hook • Arms out wide for balance • Quickness of turn and acceleration out of the turn
Progression • Work in pairs • Player X plays the ball to player O • Player O controls the ball and sprints towards the end line Progression • As soon as player O touches the ball player X chases them to try and tackle the ball away • Alternate go's	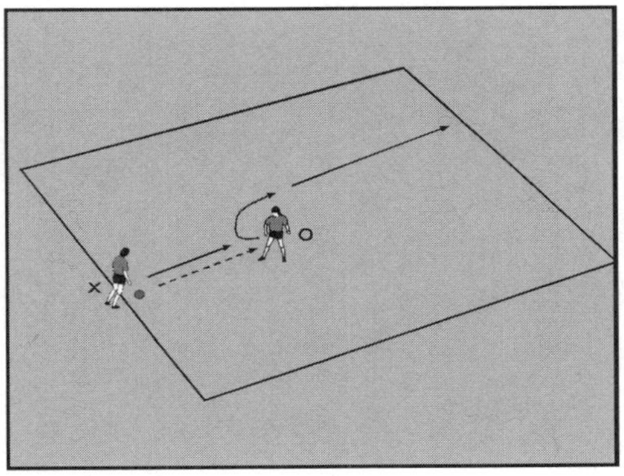	• All points listed above • Promote confidence and quickness of turn by not introducing a chasing defender until the skills are understood
Game Related Activity • Small sided (3 v 3 or 4 v 4) game • Playing area is large to promote 'getting to space' • Extra space allows the players to attempt a turn before they pass or shoot		• All points listed above • All players to attempt a turn before they pass / shoot

DEVELOPING SHOOTING

Organization	Diagram	Coaching Points
Warm Up **'Knock-out'** • All players within a rectangle • 2 players have a ball each • All other players – no ball • Players with the ball attempt to hit other players below waist height • All other players dodge the ball • Once the player has been hit they must hop out of the area		• Player with the ball must perform an accurate shot / pass • Players avoiding the ball must have their heads up to avoid collisions and the ball • Directional change – players to run forwards, sideways etc • Fake / dummy running directions / speed
Technical • Dark's & white's stand opposite each other • I ball per pair with an extra ball behind the goal • Players attempt to score past opponent from 10 yards (distance can be changed to suit age / capabilities) • Take turns alternately	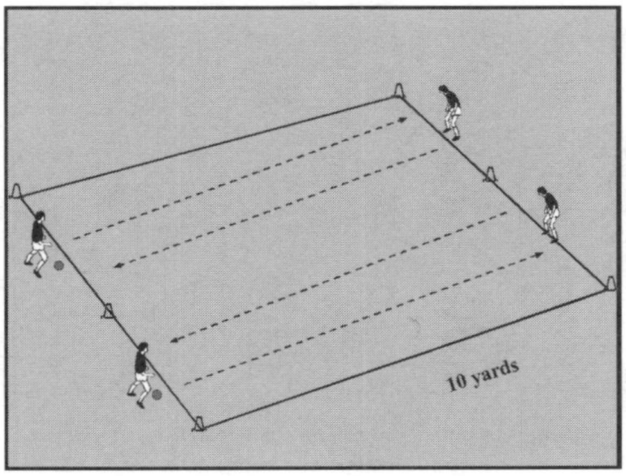	• All points above • Avoid players stopping the ball and then taking steps backwards in order to run forwards to kick the ball • Approach ball from an angle & Strike ball with the laces • Head down & eyes focused on striking the centre of the ball • Roll ball forward slightly before striking
Progression **'Hit the Corners'** • Same as above except cones are placed in each corner. • These goals promote shooting low and hard • Dark aims shot to the corners • White attempts to control and then shoots at Dark's goal • 10 points for a goal scored through the corner goals and 5 points for the centre goal • Take shot's for own goal line	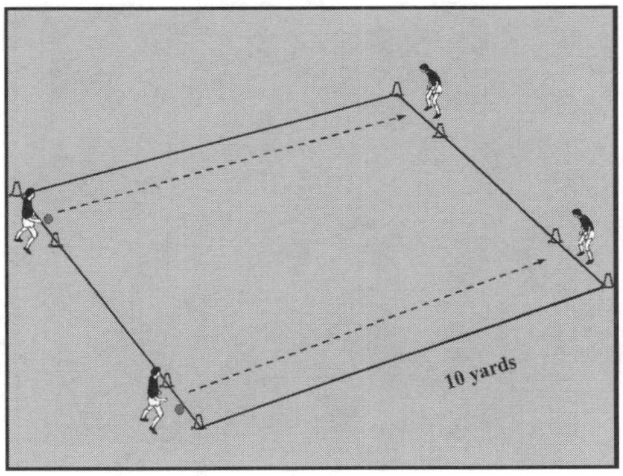	• All coaching points listed above • Advise the players to take a quick look up to see the best place to shoot. • Highlight a high /straight leg follow through
Game Related Activity • 4 v 4 game • No goal keepers • 3 teams equally matched • 1 attacker, left & right midfield players & 1 defender • Promote shape (diamond), passing and shooting • Rotate positions and teams	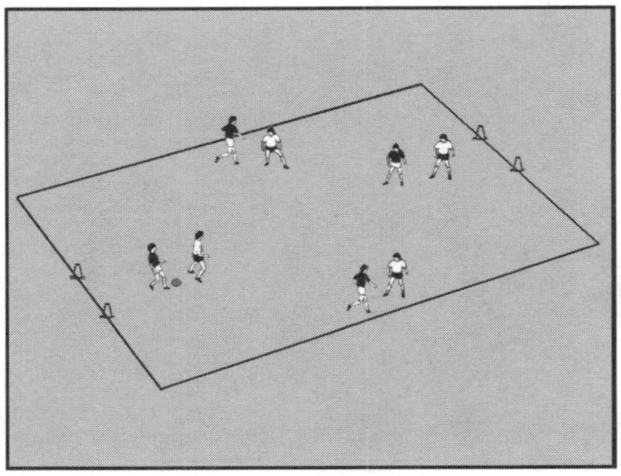	• All points listed above • Maintain positions (shape) – do not follow the ball • Pass to open players • Create space to receive the ball

Organization	Diagram	Coaching Points
Warm Up • In groups of 8, players pass short & long & follow passes • Add another ball for more touches	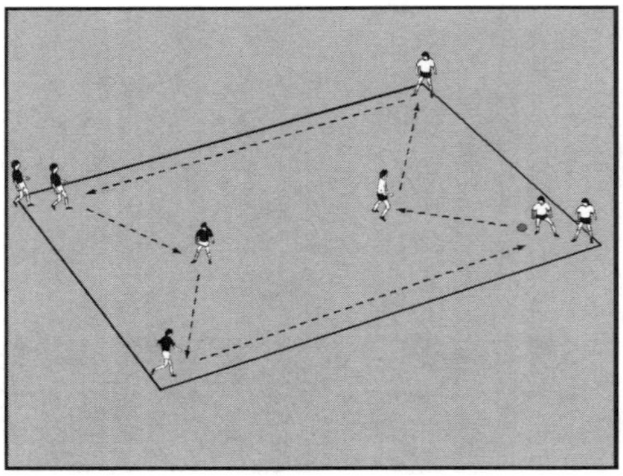	• Prepare first touch on angle for longer pass • Use laces • Keep head over ball
Technical • In groups of 8 players are organized into 4 v 4 in opposite halves • Players shoot as soon as possible when in possession		• Non kicking foot slightly behind ball • Arms out of balance
Progression • 1 defender from each team is positioned in opponents half to put pressure on shooters		• Position body to shoot in 2 touches • Strike through centre of ball
Game Related Activity • 16 players are organized into 3 v 3 in middle with 6 outside players & 2 GK's • Players must shoot after 4 passes • Rotate so that winning team stays on the field		• Identify shooting opportunities early • Hit target whenever possible.

Organization	Diagram	Coaching Points
Warm Up Players are organized into pairs. One player acts as a server the other as a 'shooter'. Players travel around the area receiving passes from various servers. Change roles		• Keeps your eye on the ball • Use the lace to make contact with the ball • Follow through to gain power
Technical Players are organized into four groups. Two groups act as servers, two as shooters. A server passes to a shooter who has an attempt on goal. Switch roles.	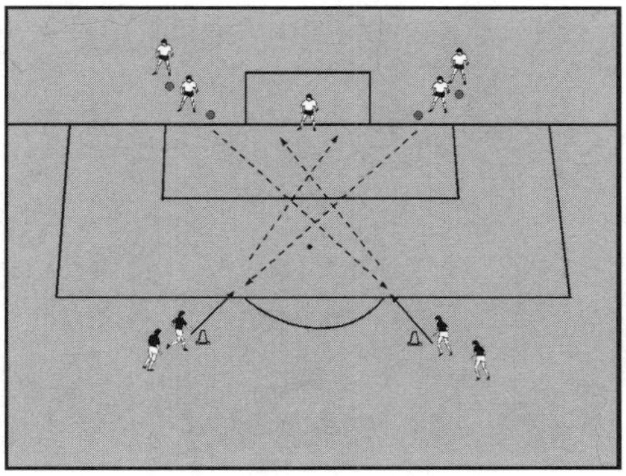	• Control the ball in the direction of the goal. • Aim for the four corners of the goal • Place your non-kicking foot further away from the ball allowing space to follow through
Progression The server now becomes a passive defender by hopping, attempting to put 'passive' pressure on the shooter.	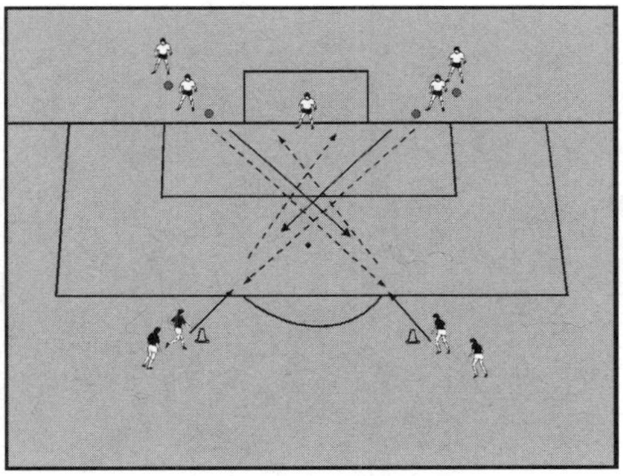	• Control the ball away from the defender • Keep your body over the ball to keep it low • Strike with the laces to gain power and direction
Game Related Activity Players are organized into pairs, with three servers around the outside of the area. Servers take it in turns to pass balls into the area. The first pair to score three goals wins.	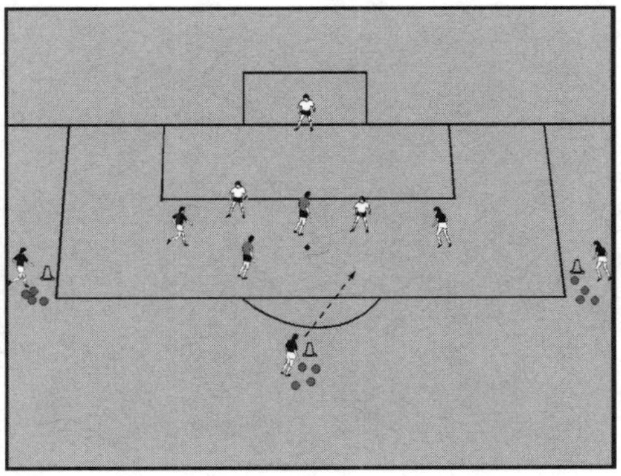	• Move to the ball quickly • Attitude - don't be afraid to shoot • Use your arms for balance

Organization	Diagram	Coaching Points
Warm Up • White's with balls dark's without. Every player has a cone. • Dark's are upside down white's are right way up. • White's have to turn dark's cones upside down whilst dribbling ball. Dark's do the opposite. • Turn into competition	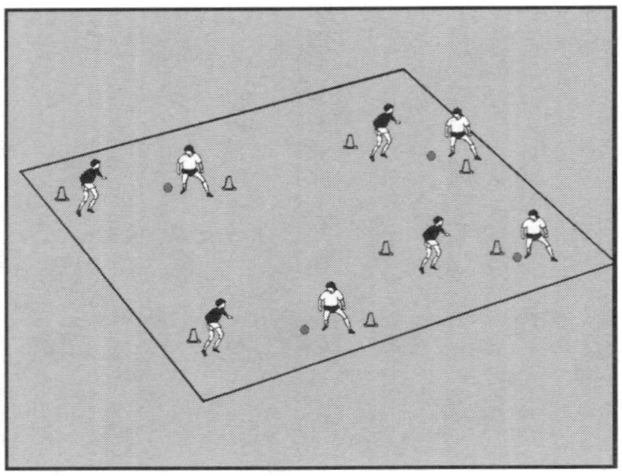	• Start slowly • Stretch • Build up speed
Technical • O1 runs out around cone in front of goal • O2 passes the ball to O1 who returns it. O1 dribbles the ball to opposite end and shoots. • X's repeat 1) X's and O's go at the same time – race to score goal first	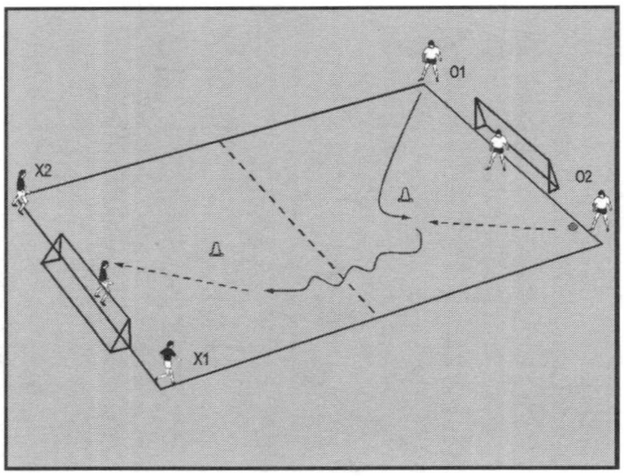	• Ball out of feet • Accuracy • Pace
Progression • As above • O's go 1st and X1 & X2 defend (X1 must wait until O1 receives ball back before they can defend) • Progress to 2 v 2	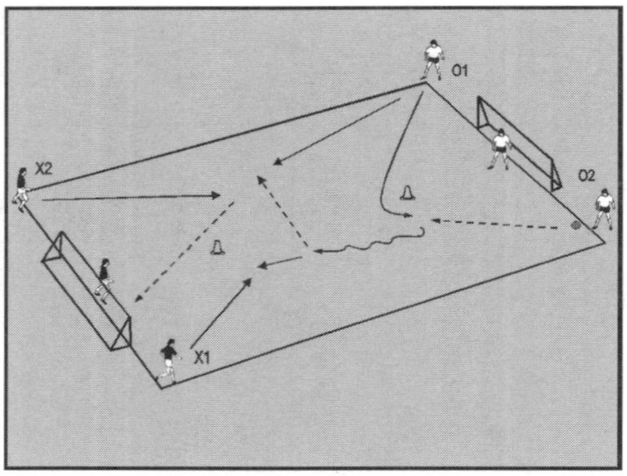	• When to shoot • Head over ball • Use laces / side foot
Game Related Activity • Dark's v White's • 3 goals to score at each end. • 2 points for the middle, 1 either side	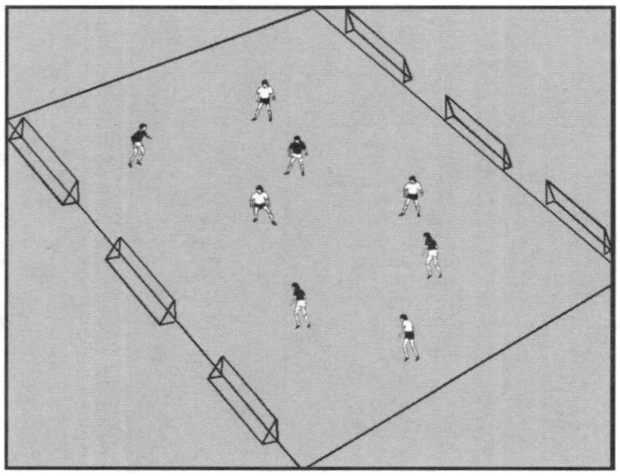	• Shoot when ever possible • Laces / side foot • Accuracy/pace

DEVELOPING DEFENDING

<table>
<tr><th>Organization</th><th>Diagram</th><th>Coaching Points</th></tr>
<tr><td>Warm Up
Players have a ball between two. The player with the ball dribbles around the area. The partner shadows the dribbler. Change roles.</td><td></td><td>• Keep your eyes on the ball
• Bend your knees to help change direction
• Stay close to your partner</td></tr>
<tr><td>Technical
Players are organized into pairs in a 10 x 10 area. X1 passes to O1 and attempts to defend the end line. Switch roles.</td><td>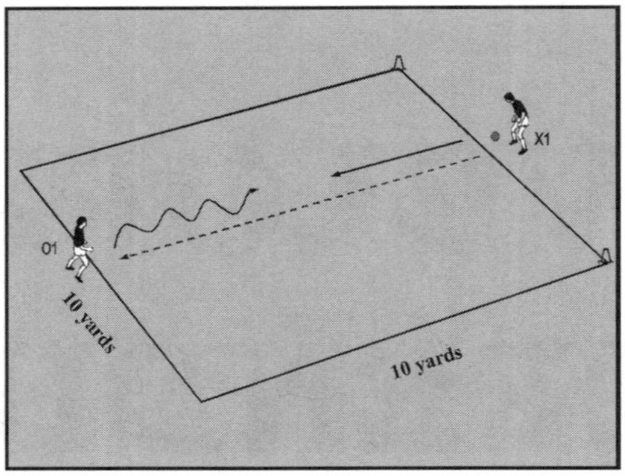
</td><td>• Pressure the ball by moving towards it quickly.
• Slow down as you approach the attacker.
• Bend your knees to allow you to change direction</td></tr>
<tr><td>Progression
Players are organized into pairs. X1 + X2 pass to O1 + O2 and attempt to defend the end line. Switch roles.</td><td>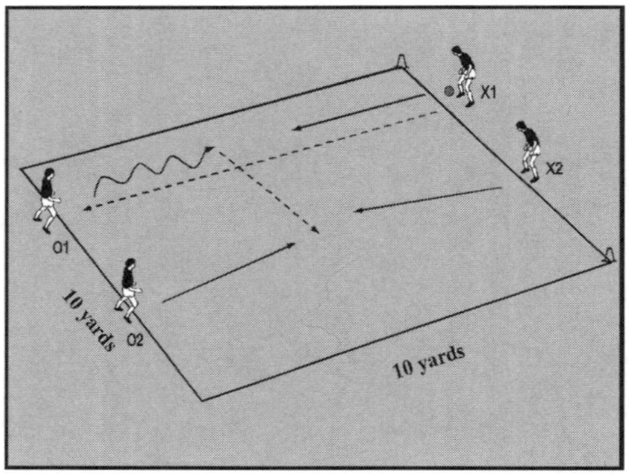
</td><td>• The nearest defender puts pressure on the ball
• The second defender provides cover and support
• Communicate with each other to help you work together</td></tr>
<tr><td>Game Related Activity
The group is organized into two teams. One team defends a small central goal. The second team defends two wide goals</td><td>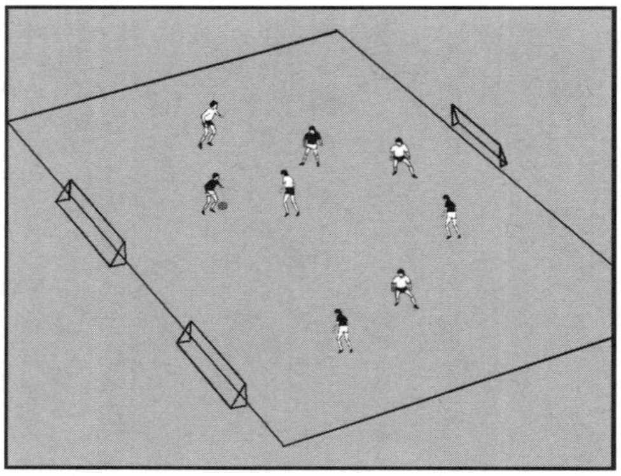</td><td>• Show compact as a team to close down space
• Be patient when tackling</td></tr>
</table>

Organization	Diagram	Coaching Points
Warm Up • In pairs • Dark's with balls white's without. • Dark's dribble white's always have to get in front of ball	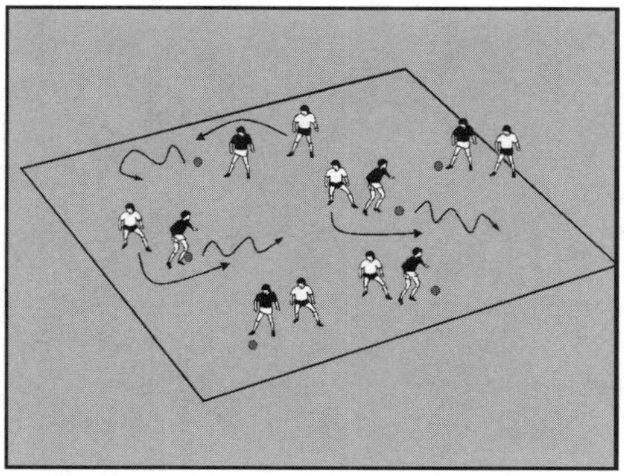	• Short feet movement • Side on • Always in front of ball
Technical • In 4's • 1 v 1. Dark's have to try and dribble the ball into goal in the corner of the area. • White's have to try and stop them. • Alternate attacker and defender	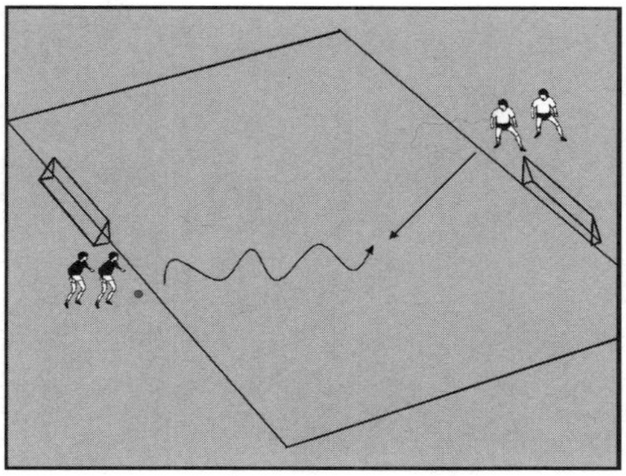	• Close down ball • Encourage attacker away from goal • Last thing is to tackle
Progression • As above turn into 2 v 2	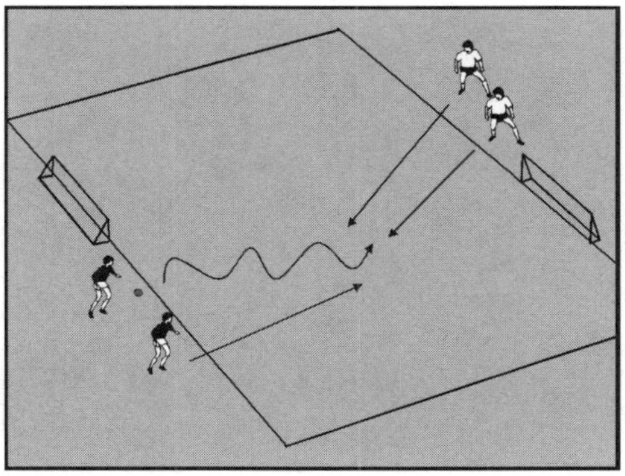	• Defenders work together • One closes other offers cover • Last thing tackle
Game Related Activity • Dark's v White's • Each team has 2 wide goals to score in.		• Show away from danger area • One player closes ball • More defenders than attackers

Organization	Diagram	Coaching Points
Warm Up • In 2's players follow/lead each other around area with 1 ball • 1 player moves forward with ball, other backwards	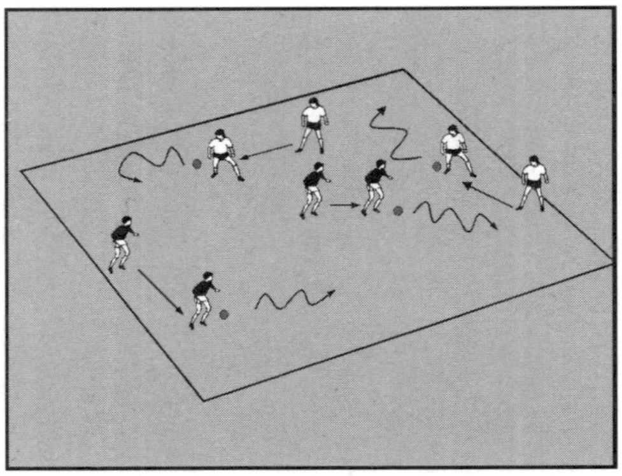	• Spacial Awareness • Light on toes • Don't allow ball to pass
Technical • 16 players are split into 4 groups of 4 in each corner • Upon command players play 1 v 1	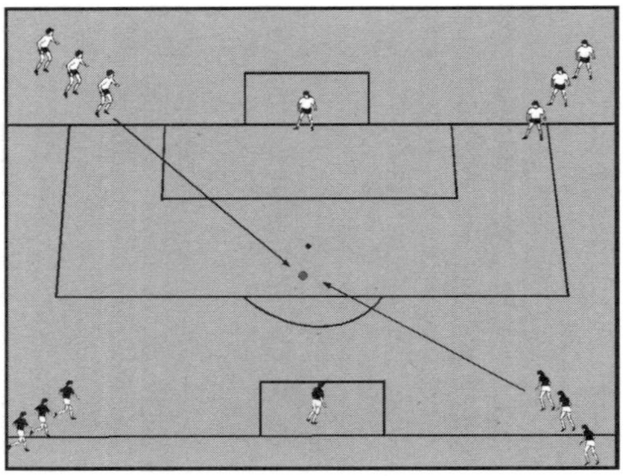	• Close space between player & ball • Lead with nearest foot
Progression • Repeat activity changing commands to : 2 v 1, 2 v 2	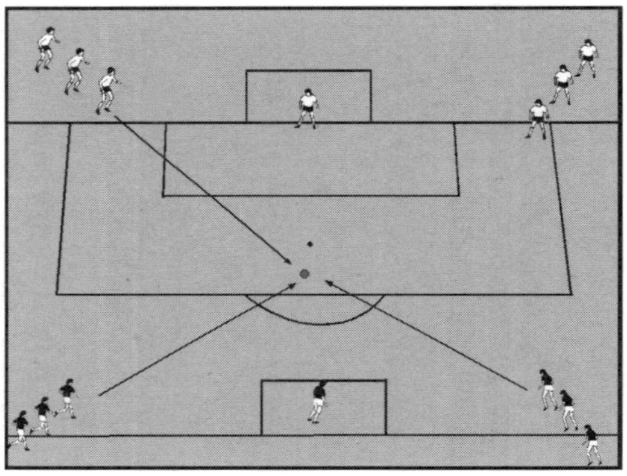	• Angle body to "cut off" opponent • Force play away from goal
Game Related Activity • 8 players play 4 v 4 • When team is not in possession, all players must move into own half.		• As above

DEVELOPING GOALKEEPING

Organization	Diagram	Coverage Points
Warm Up • Dark's with balls White's without. • Players with balls run around bouncing and catching the ball, avoiding players without the ball. • Upon command dark's roll ball to white's. 1) Bounce the ball to white's 2) Catch without bounce		• Ball familiarization • Get in line with ball • Use two hands to collect ball • Have fun - get muddy
Technical • In 2's players stand opposite each other. • Dark throws/rolls the ball to white. White has to gather ball and return it. 1) Players on knees 2) Players standing		• Get in line with ball • Collect ball into chest • Body behind ball • Keep legs closed
Progression • Players push the ball back and forth to cones. • Gk has to stretch to save ball. • Players on knees / standing. 1) Players try and score past each other (ball must stay on ground) 2) 2 v 2	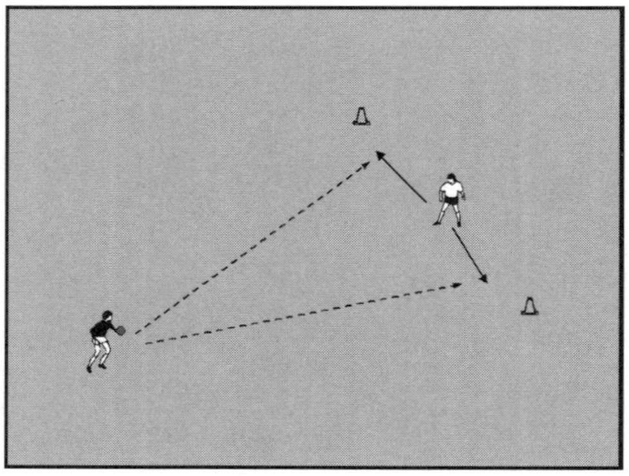	• Spread finger tips • Quick movements • Body behind ball
Game Related Activity • 2 teams. • Feet are not allowed to be used. • Ball passed around by either over arm or rolling. • To score the attacking team must throw the ball into the coned area and be caught by one of their players. • To score a bonus point the attacking team can have a free shot at knocking the ball off the cone, which is outside the coned area (roll / over arm)		• Watch ball • Type of throw • Body behind ball

Organization	Diagram	Coaching Points
Warm Up Players travel around a designated area. Three balls are passed from to player randomly. Players are not allowed to stand still.		• Keep your eye on the ball • Try to get both hands on the ball • Serve the ball in different ways to the next player
Technical Players are organized into three groups. Each player takes a turn to shoot at the goalkeeper. Switch the goalkeeper	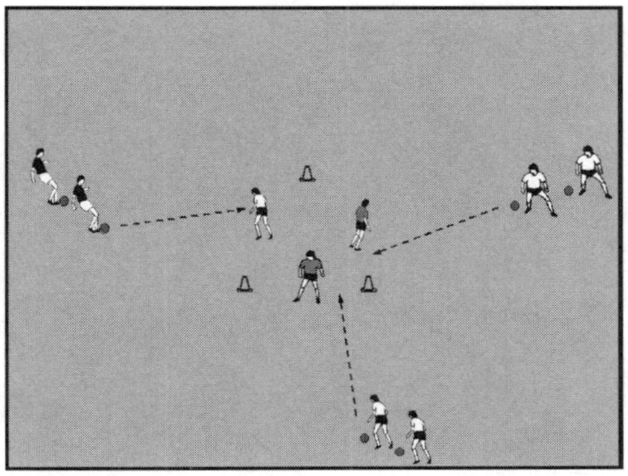	• Get in line with the ball • Move your feet to get closer to the ball • Protect the ball by bringing it into the body
Progression Shoot to score. Change groups in a clockwise direction	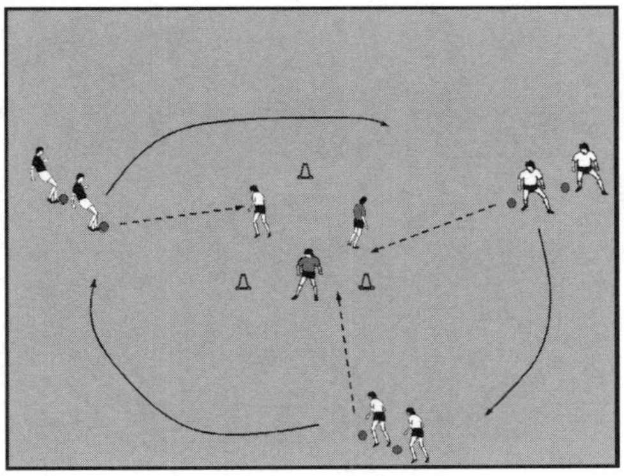	• Keep your hands up in a 'ready' position • Bend your knees to allow quick movement • Move towards the ball to narrow the angle
Game Related Activity Players are organized into two teams. Teams must use their hands to move the ball. Score by throwing the ball into the opponents goal		• Move the ball quickly • Keep your eye on the ball • Collect the ball at it's highest point when served high • Use high knee lift to gain more jumping height

Organization	Diagram	Coaching Points
Warm Up • 16 players form 4 groups of 4 throwing & catching to next line clockwise. • Follow throw to end of next line • Alternate moving clockwise and anti-clockwise	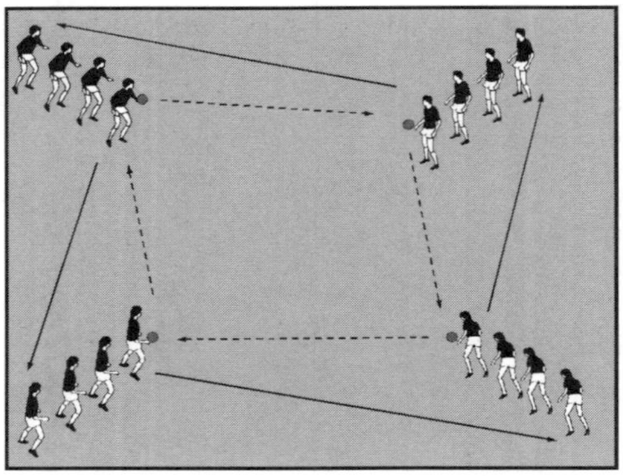	• Move in line with ball • Keep eye on ball • Catch with 2 hands and bring to chest
Technical • In 4's sitting together with legs astride players throw ball across square. • Players prevent ball from going past them		• Fixed/stiff wrists • Remain upright • Keep eye on ball
Progression • In 4's (1 server, 3 GK's) players react to service once in middle of goal • Rotate & repeat, varying service.	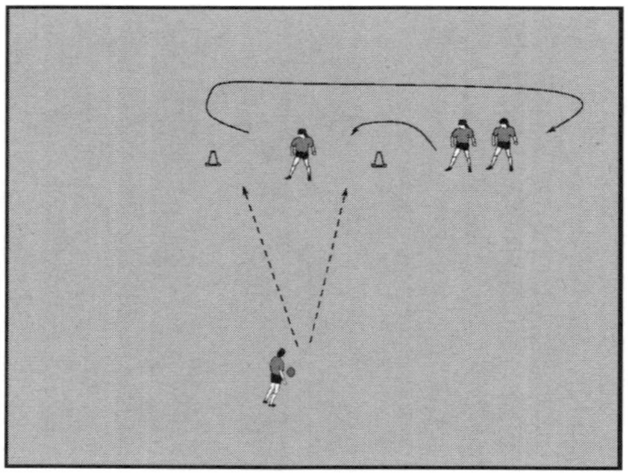	• Light on toes • Dive to remain in forward position • Get body behind ball
Game Related Activity • 8 players (4 GK's 2 x X's, 2 O's) • Players can score in any goal • Rotate GK's every 2 minutes		• As above

Organization	Diagram	Coaching Points
Warm Up • All players have a ball and stay within the area • On the command Go players move around the area throwing the ball into the air • The ball may bounce once before catching • Half the group have a ball and the other half do not • In one minute how many times can each player receive a thrown pass and catch it before it hits the ground.		• Eyes wide open and 'watch' the ball into the arms • Arms outstretched to receive the ball • Avoid collisions
Technical • Players work in 2's • 2 cones 5 yards apart • Player 1 (feeder) rolls the ball along the ground and aims for the corner of the goal • Player 2 (goalkeeper) starts by kneeling and makes their body fall sideways to block the ball • Alternate after ten attempts each	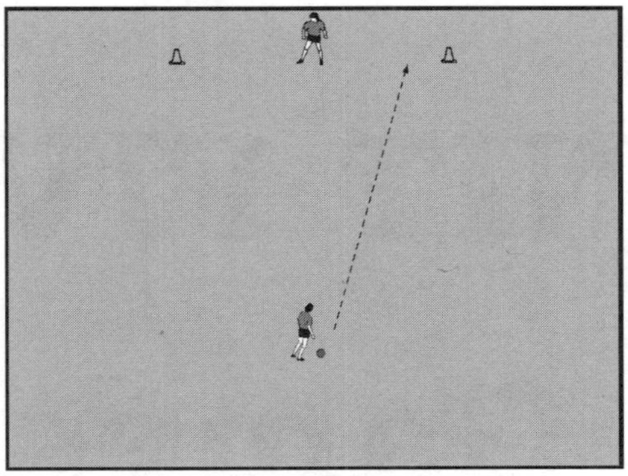	• All points above • The 'diving player must attempt to get their chest to act as a barrier to the ball • Crouch (bend knees) and dive when possible • Feeder must feed the ball underarm and at a good pace to help the goalkeeper learn
Progression • Players work in groups of three • 2 balls per group • Players 1 & 2 stand at opposite ends with the goalkeeper in between. • Players 1 & 2 alternate shots at the goal keeper • Goalkeeper faces player one for the first shot and then player 2 for the second (continue) • Every player has twenty shots – count how many are saved	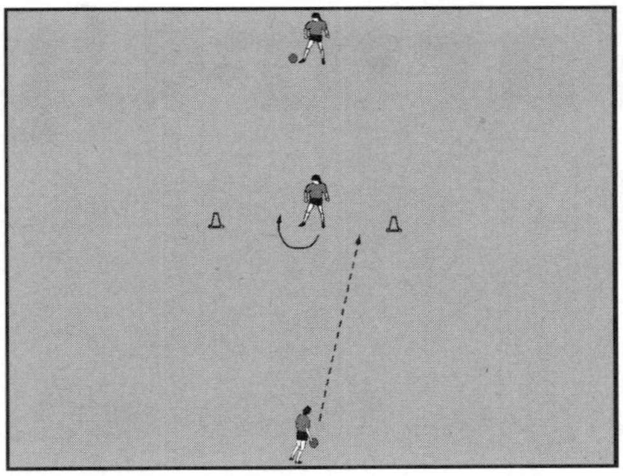	• All points above • Goalkeeper moves sideways into the line of the ball • Hands outstretched to receive the ball • Attempt to get the ball into the chest area • Crouch (bend knees) and dive when possible
Game Related Activity • Four goals and a goalkeeper in each goal • Teams can score in any goal • Small area creates more scoring opportunities • Change goalkeepers regularly		• All points above • Goalkeepers remain on their toes • Good handling and movement into the line of the ball is required. • Crouch (bend knees) and dive when possible

UNIT FIVE

Fun Games For Warm-Ups

Organization	Diagram	Progressions/Variations
Target Ball Split the group into two teams. Each player has a ball. Place each team at opposite end lines and place a number of balls balanced on cones. On the coach's command players can begin passing. The objective is to knock all balls off their opponents cones before their opponents knock off yours. Each player must retrieve his/her own ball.	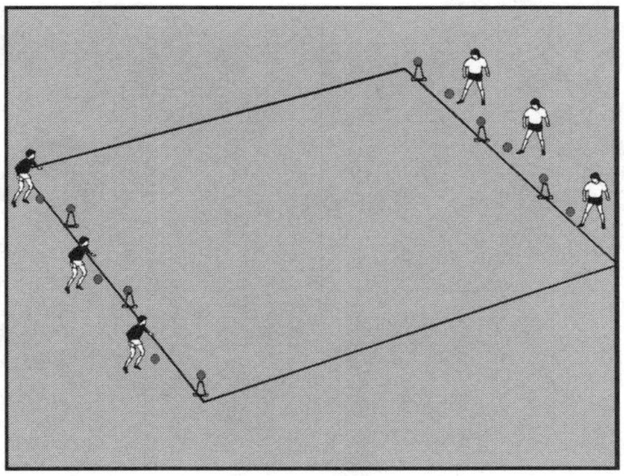	If there are not enough balls, put players on the line with the objective now being to pass a ball through his/her legs.
Free Movement Each player begins by standing next to a disk. One disk per player. To begin, players simply jog in any direction moving from one disk to the next. Player movements can be color coded ensuring that he plots a course through the web following the same color disk at which they started.	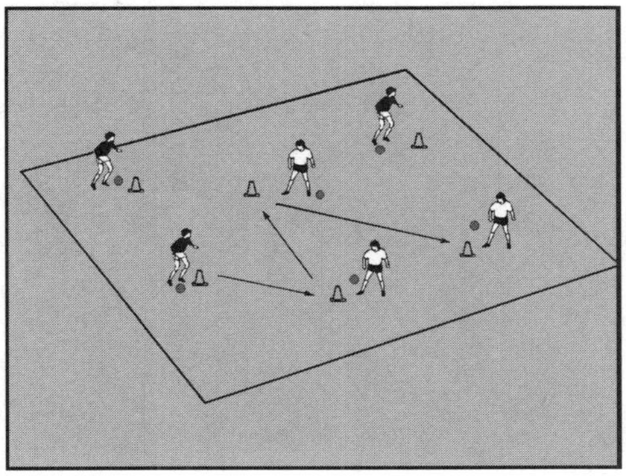	• Players can perform various activities when arriving at each disk: running side to side, running backwards, skipping etc • Other activities can be introduced: touch the disk, jump up, complete a spin etc • Keep eye on ball • Experience travelling with the ball
Nutmeg Competition Place players in a confined area. Half the group have a ball each. The other group find a space and stand with their legs apart. The group with the balls have sixty seconds to score as many 'nutmegs' as possible. After sixty seconds switch roles.		• Dribble with head up • Awareness of others
Sharks Place the players in a defined area. Each player has a ball. Players are eliminated if they fail to keep the ball within the defined area. As well as defending their own ball, the players are encouraged to kick other balls out of the area. Players can only eliminate others whilst they are still in the game.		• As above

Organization	Diagram	Progressions/Variations
Crabs and Fish Split the group into two. Designate one group as the "Crabs" and station them without balls anywhere in the central area. The second group are the "Fishes" stationed in the end zone, and on the coaches command, the fishes have to dribble to the opposite end of the area without being caught by a crab. If caught they leave their ball and become a crab. Continue until all fishes are caught then switch roles.	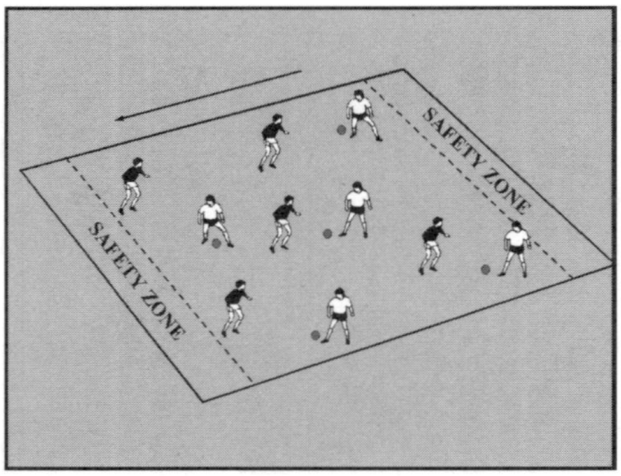	• Close control • Keep eye on ball • Awareness of others and space
Dodge Ball Organize two teams, one within a defined area, the other team surrounding them. The team on the outside have a ball each and try to hit players on the inside. Players are eliminated if they are hit below the waist.	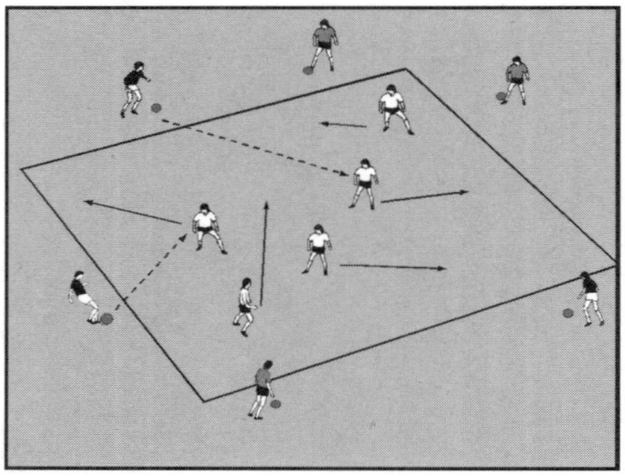	**Variations and Progressions** • Five Gears of a Car: When the coach shouts out the gear of a car, e.g. "3rd Gear", the player must vary the speed of his dribbling accordingly. • "Traffic Lights": Red = Stop, Amber = Tap dance on the ball, Green = Go • Stop and Change (Balls) • "Colored Cones": Players race to a cone of that color
Continuous Football Cricket Split the group into two teams. Only one ball is needed. One team will "bat" first whilst the other team "fields". A bowler (normally the coach) passes the ball trying to knock down the three cones (wicket). A batsman kicks the ball forward using only the inside of the foot. He then tries to score a run by running around a cone which is place either side of him. The ball is returned to the bowler who may bowl before the batsman returns.	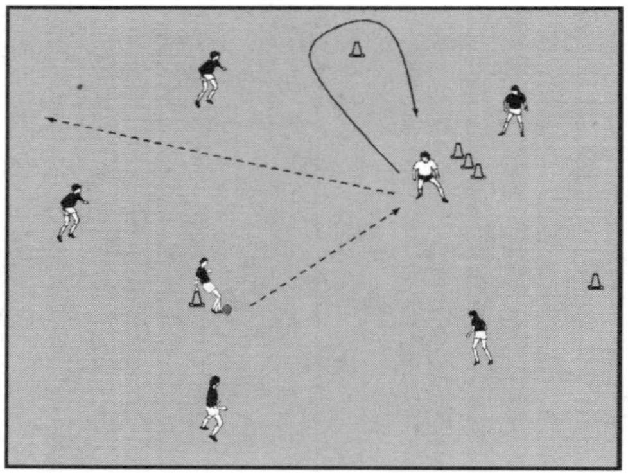	**Rules:** You are deemed "out" if: • the ball hits the wicket • you are caught by a fielder • Use another part of your body other than the instep to "hit" the ball • Three players "out" means the end of a teams innings
British Bulldog To begin, select one player to be "The Bulldog" and position him/her in the middle of the area without a ball. Position all other players with a ball at one end of the area. On the coaches command the players must try to get to the opposite end. If tackled by the Bulldog, you automatically become a bulldog too.	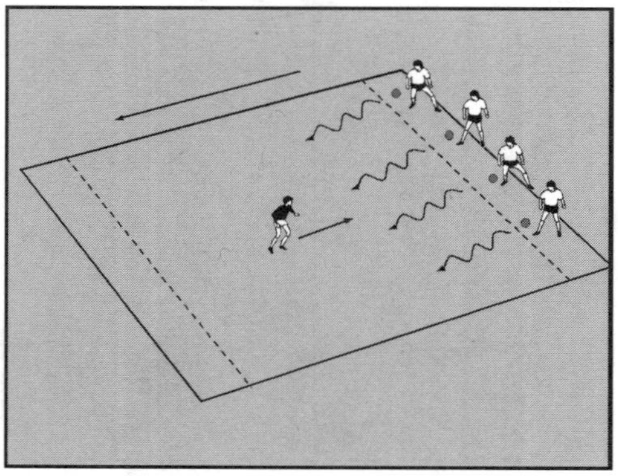	• Close control • Keep eye on ball • Awareness of others and space

Organization	Diagram	Progressions/Variations
Chain Tag One player is designated as the "Tagger". If the Tagger tags another player then they join hands to make a chain. They continue to tag ('chain up') until there is four, then they split into two pairs and so on.		
Throw/Head/Catch Split the group into two teams and place them in a confined area. Using cones, make two goals at either end of the field. Players must keep the ball by working in a sequence. The person who has the ball must "throw" the ball to a team-mate. The receiving player must then "head" the ball back to the server or another team-mate. He/she must then "catch" the ball.		Rules: The defending team can only gain possession by intercepting the ball by using the correct part of the sequence. The only other way to gain possession is if the ball goes out of play or is missed by the attacking team. As a progression you can only score through a diving header.
"Strike" Split the group into two teams. Each player has a ball. Place each team at opposite ends facing each other. In the middle of the area, in between both teams, place a "marked ball". On the coaches' command players can begin passing. The objective is to strike the marked ball and push it over the opponents end line.	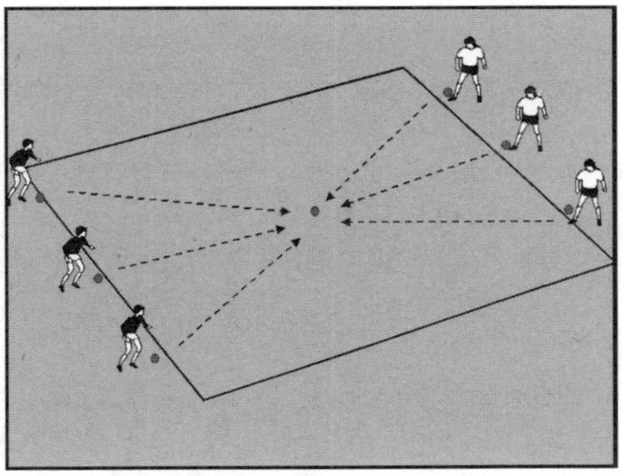	• Quality of pass • Accuracy of pass • Weight of pass
Individual Activities with the Ball Allow players to move freely within a designated area then give them a number of skill challenges to complete as part of their warm up.	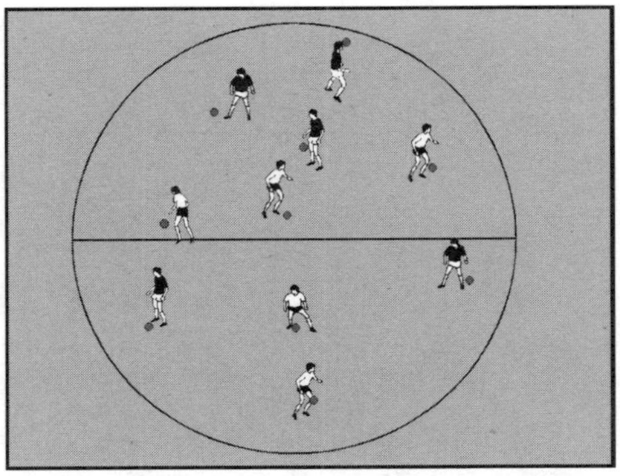	• Tap dancing, Keep ups, Drag backs, Pull back and change direction, using the sole of the foot, inside and outsides, heel to toes, inside both feet, etc.

Organization	Diagram	Progressions/Variations
Wild Animals All players are given a ball each. Players dribble within a defined area. Three players start on the outside of the area and do not have balls. These players are the "wild animals". On the coaches command they enter the area and attempt to kick players balls out of the area. If you lose your ball you become a "wild animal" also.	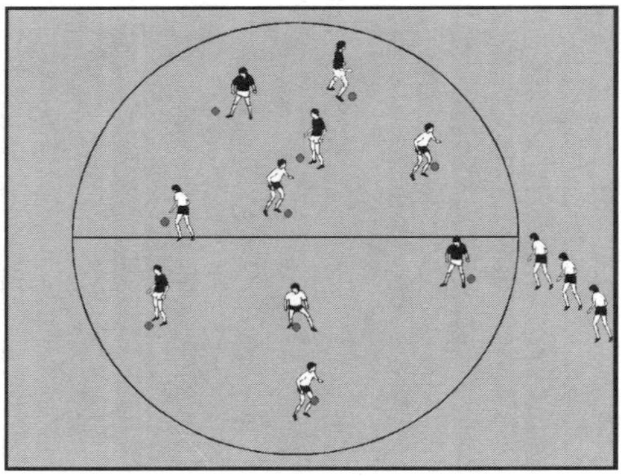	• Continue until nobody remains with a ball
Team Run Four teams. One ball per team. Place all the balls in a central area with each player sitting/standing around or outside the area. Players react to their number being called by collecting a ball, travelling around a cone placed on the outside and returning to the start.	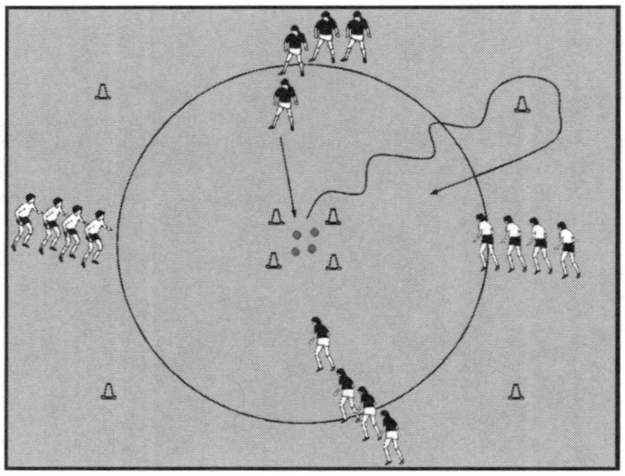	• Players can be asked to travel/ dribble around any number of cones • Allow more players to travel/ dribble at the same time by placing more balls to the central area
"Top" Three All the players have a ball. Set out three squares big enough for the group all to fit inside. Simply give each square a name, i.e Liverpool, Arsenal and Manchester United, these are your top three! Start all players in the center of the area and shout out a name. The first player to reach the square in control of his/her ball is the winner and gets to choose the next team to visit.	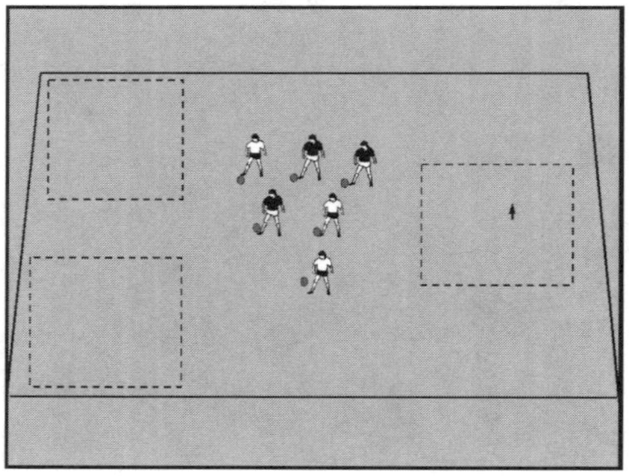	• Ensure that the squares are placed far enough apart to ensure players dribble the ball
American Shoot-Out Split the group into two teams. Give each group a team name. To begin, position one team behind the goal to retrieve balls. That team chooses one player to go in goal. Position the second team behind a set of cones 20-25 yards from goal, with a ball each. On the coaches command, the team with the balls have 60 seconds to score as many goals as possible.	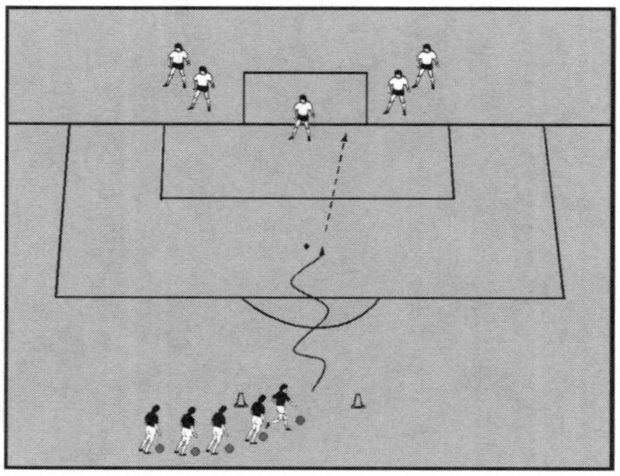	• The next player can only go after a goal is scored or a save is made

Organization	Diagram	Progressions/Variations
Planets Four teams. As many balls as possible. Place all the balls in the center of the area being used. On the coaches command, one player from each team collects one ball at a time and returns it to his planet. The team with most balls after sixty seconds is the winner.	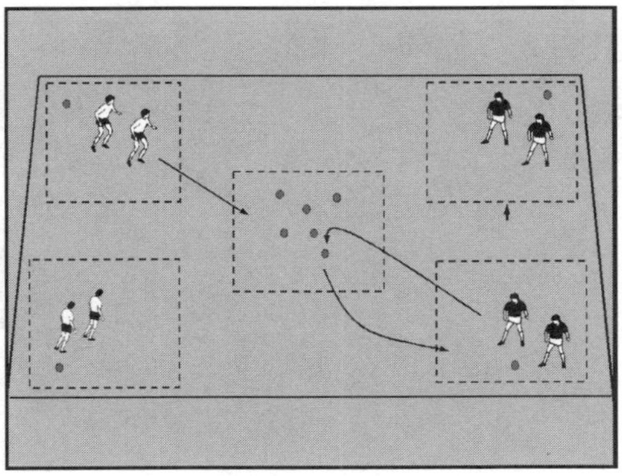	• As well as collecting from the central area, progress to allow the players to collect balls from opponents planets also
Follow the Leader Plaće sets of different colored cones two yards apart in a designated area. Put players into pairs, one is the leader, the other the follower. The leader leads the follower through cones to score as many goals as possible in sixty seconds. Change roles.	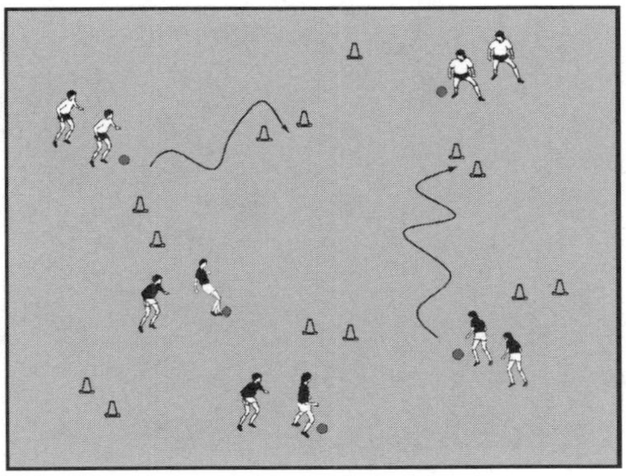	• With or without a ball • As a progression, one partner must defend the other to score • In pairs the leader attempts to score upon the command of a different color
Rabbits Tails Within a confined area each player is given a bib to be placed in the back of their shorts The bibs should be "sticking out" as if it were a tail. On the shout of "go" each player attempts to grab as many bibs tails as possible without losing their own tail.		• Light on toes • Quick decision making • Speed
Race Against Time Two teams of players. One ball per group. Players on the black team pass against the coach/or a wall and count how many passes they can make. The length of time allowed is determined by the time it takes each player from the white team to dribble a ball around the 'working group' and back to the start position.	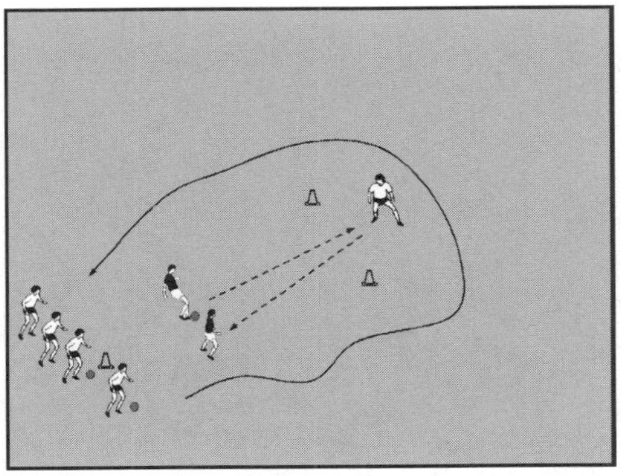	• Speed of the dribble • Accuracy of the pass • Team work

Organization	Diagram	Progressions/Variations
Marbles Football Position players within a defined area. Each player has a ball. Place two players in bibs. These players are "on". On the coaches command all players dribble around the area. All players who are not in bibs must attempt to shoot at and strike the dribblers with their own ball. The player who is on protects his/her ball by dribbling randomly within the area. Players take it in turns to be on.	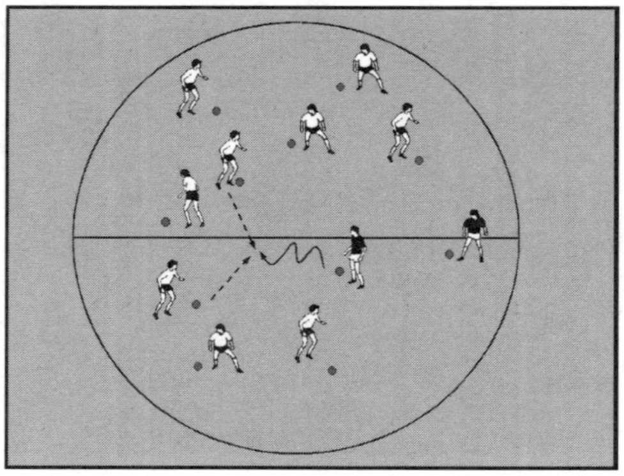	• Add more "on" players • Reduce the playing space

UNIT SIX

Mini-Soccer Guidelines

WHY PLAY MINI-SOCCER?

1. There is more contact with the ball leading to **better technique**. In 11 v 11 the ratio of ball to outfield players is 1: 20. Because there are fewer players in Mini-Soccer, each player has more contact with the ball which helps technical development.
2. There is more contact with the ball leading to more participation and, usually, **more enjoyment**. Success is easier to achieve.
3. Because the ball is never far away from the player, the chance of **developing concentration** is greatly increased. Playing 11-a-side soccer, many children lose interest in the game because the ball goes out of their immediate vicinity and they quickly become 'bored' spectators.
4. **Decision making** is easier because of the small numbers involved. As a result, the players will gain a **greater understanding** of the game. Basic soccer situations are easier to see and simpler to solve.
5. Fewer players, more space and simpler decisions will encourage **more movement** of players whatever the situation.

FOR COACHES
Mini-Soccer is

- easy to organize
- for boys and girls of all abilities, including the disabled
- a game played anywhere, anytime
- a more appropriate activity than 11-a-side soccer

MINI-SOCCER IS THE BASIS OF ALL SOCCER
Small-sided games have been played for hundreds of years in the street, the playground, or on the beach and many professional teams use them as the basis for their coaching. They invariably lead to basic soccer situations, such as 3 v 3, 4 v 4 and 5 v 5 so typical of the 11-a-side game.

Mini-Soccer, through its dynamic tempo, produces more vigorous exercise than 11-a-side soccer and so helps to improve children's fitness levels.

TO ORGANIZE MINI-SOCCER YOU WILL NEED

- any level surface on which it is suitable to play soccer
- a ball, no larger than Size 4. Size 3 is recommended for under 8's two goals, 12 ft x 6 ft if you don't have a set of goals, use cones or marker discs, 12 ft apart
- the children to wear training shoes or soccer boots if the surface is wet
- markings laid out with the use of lines, marker discs or cones

- **There should be no debris or dangerous hazards either on the field of play or in the immediate surrounding area. A conventional soccer field can easily be converted to Mini-Soccer. This can also minimize wear of the central areas of the playing field. Corner flags may be used as goals but must be at least five feet high and have a non-pointed top.**

- **The general aim is to provide a safe, supervised environment for children to enjoy their introduction to Soccer.**

- **There should be no knock-out competitions or leagues involving Mini Soccer : the game itself will be a sufficient challenge for the children.**

DIMENSIONS OF A MINI-SOCCER FIELD

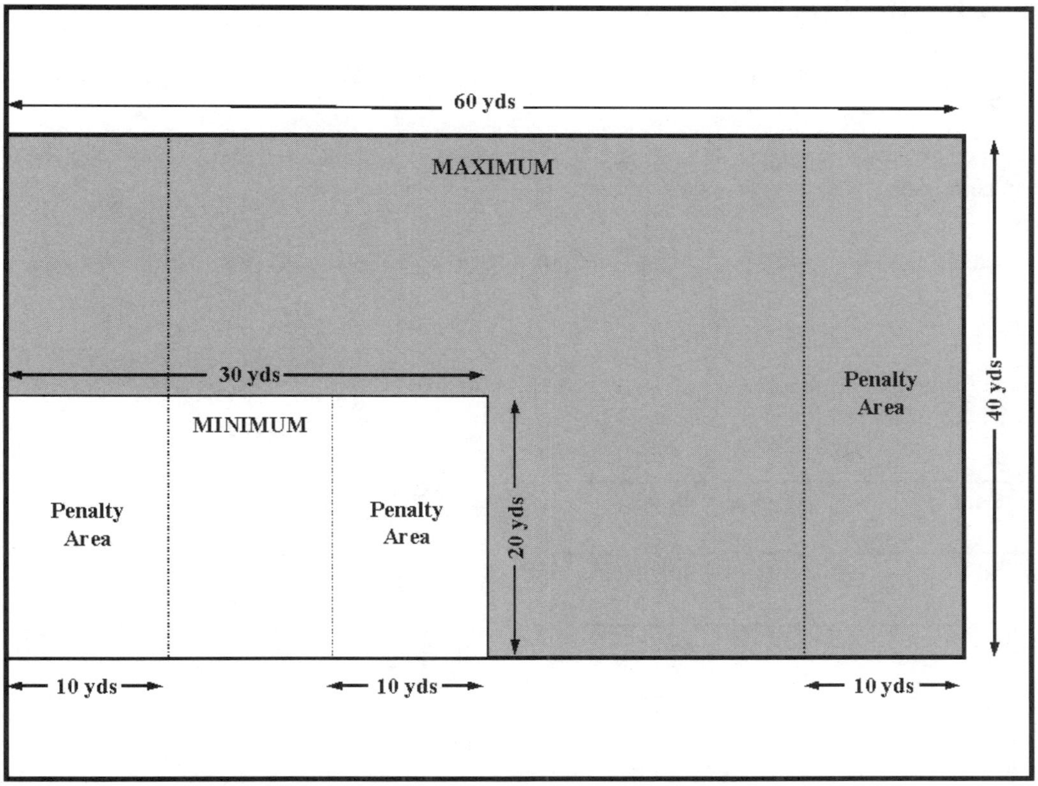

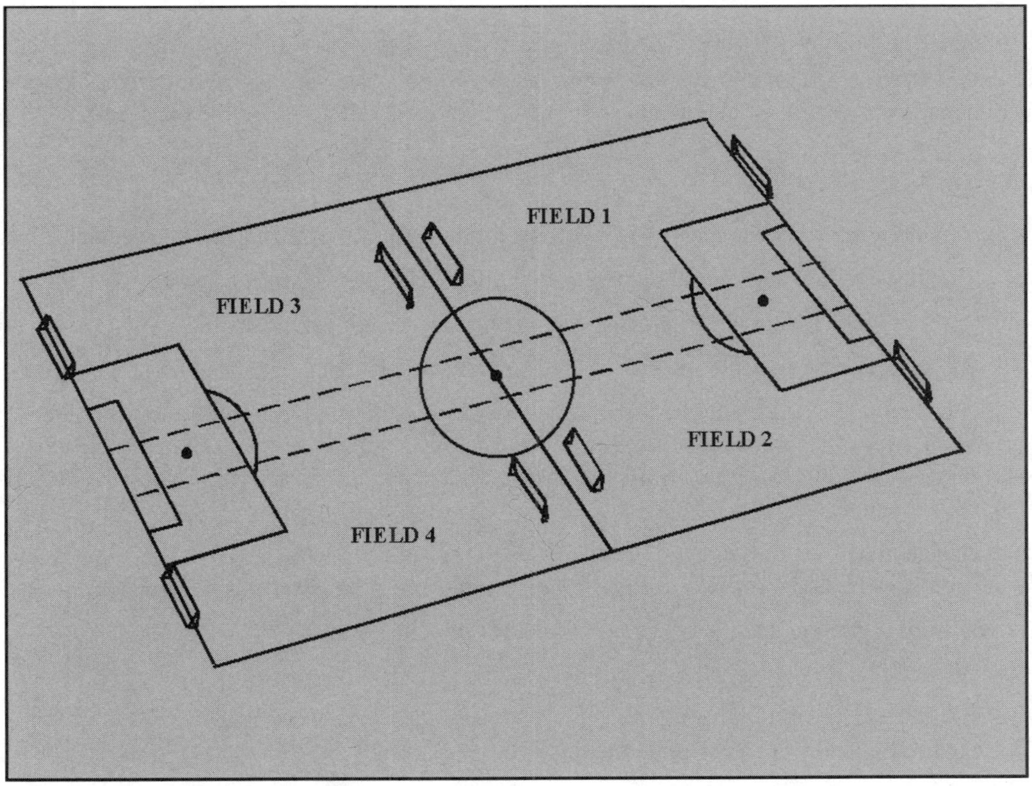

THE RULES OF MINI-SOCCER

- The rules are simple and as near to real soccer as possible . A game leader who is urged to be as flexible with the youngest children, supervises the matches.
- Rules are explained as the game proceeds (for example, hand ball, and then in/out of play). It may also be necessary to demonstrate in certain instances how to restart the game (e.g. throw-in, corner kicks).

- The game is for boys and girls aged 5 to 11 (as of midnight 31st August the previous year) and mixed soccer is allowed in all the age ranges.
- Laws 9 and 10 apply to mini soccer but there is no off-side.
- Team size should be no greater than 7 v 7. The playing area should be no greater than 60 yds x 40 yds and no smaller than 30 yds x 20 yds. Team and playing area sizes are recommended as follows:

Under 11, 10 years **7 v 7**	**60 yds x 40 yds**
Under 9, 8 years **5 v 5**	**50 yds x 30 yds**
Under 7, 6 **4 v 4**	**40 yds x 30 yds**

- Any number of substitutes may be used at any time with the permission of the game leader. Players may re-enter the game and all substitutes must have a period of play. As far as possible there should be equal playing time for each player.
- The ball should be no larger than size 4. Size 3 is recommended for under 6's and 7's. Players are required to wear shinguards.
- The recommended goal size for all age groups is 12 ft x 6 ft.
- The goal area extends 10 yards from the goal line across the full width of the playing area regardless of its size. The goal area can either be marked by cones on the touchline or one or two marker discs across the playing area.
- Each game should last for a maximum of 20 minutes. Half time need not be taken. Games of 10 minutes in total are recommended for the younger players.
- The kick off is taken in the centre of the playing area to start the game and after a goal has been scored.
- Although Law 15 applies and the throw in should be taken in the normal way, game leaders can show flexibility.
- Law 17 applies to corner kicks except the opposition should be at least three yards away.
- Law 12 applies to free kicks although they area all indirect and the opposition should be at least three yards away.
- Goalkeepers can, (1) handle the ball in the penalty area and there are no restrictions on the number of steps they may take when holding the ball, (2) cannot handle the ball outside the penalty area under 6's, 7's, 8's and 9's may kick the ball out of their hands and under 10's and 11's are only allowed to throw the ball, (3) can kick the ball on the ground but may then be challenged by opponents.
- Goal-kicks are taken anywhere on the edge of the penalty area - the opposition should be at least 3 yards away.must be kicked out of the goal area by under 6's, 7' s, 8's and 9's may be taken from their hands from within the goal area.
- There are no restrictions regarding the number of players allowed in the goal area.
- Players can pass the ball to their own goalkeeper, for the goalkeeper to handle the ball.

Laws of the game can be obtained from any Soccer National Governing Body